2001

Mutual Fund Fact Book

41st Edition

A guide to *trends*

and *statistics* in the

mutual fund industry

INVESTMENT COMPANY INSTITUTE®

Forty-first Edition

ISBN 1-878731-30-0

Copyright © 2001 by Investment Company Institute

About ICI

The Investment Company Institute (ICI) is the national association of the investment company industry. Its mission is to advance the interests of investment companies (mutual funds, closed-end funds, and unit investment trusts) and their shareholders, to promote public understanding of investment companies, and to serve the public interest by encouraging adherence to high ethical standards by all elements of the business. As the only association of U.S. investment companies without regard to distribution method or affiliation, the Institute is dedicated to the interests of the entire investment company industry and all of its shareholders. The Institute represents members and their shareholders before legislative and regulatory bodies at both the federal and state levels, spearheads investor awareness initiatives, disseminates industry information to the public and the media, provides economic policy and other policy research, and seeks to maintain high industry standards.

The association was originally formed by industry leaders who supported the enactment of the Investment Company Act of 1940, legislation that provided the strong regulatory structure that has been responsible for much of the industry's success. Established in New York in 1940 as the National Committee of Investment Companies, the association was renamed the National Association of Investment Companies in 1941 and the Investment Company Institute in 1961. The Institute was relocated to Washington, DC in 1970.

Table of Contents

List of Figures

CHAPTER 4

Mutual Fund Ownership and Shareholder Characteristics

CHAPTER 5

Mutual Funds and the Retirement Market

CHAPTER 1

Features of Mutual Funds

A mutual fund is an investment company that pools money from shareholders and invests in a diversified portfolio of securities. Mutual fund investors buy fund shares that represent ownership in all of the fund's securities.

Variety

There are four basic types of mutual funds: stock (also called equity), money market, bond, and hybrid. Money market funds are referred to as short-term funds because they invest in securities that generally mature in about one year or less, while stock, bond, and hybrid funds are known as long-term funds. (Hybrid funds invest in a combination of stocks, bonds, and other securities.) Of the total $6.97 trillion invested in mutual funds at the end of 2000, $3.96 trillion was invested in stock funds, $1.85 trillion in money market funds, $808 billion in bond funds, and $350 billion in hybrid funds.

At the end of 2000, about 8,200 mutual funds were available to investors, offering a wide variety of investment objectives, from conservative to aggressive, and investing in a wide range of securities. The Investment Company Institute classifies mutual funds into 33 broad categories according to their basic investment objective (see pages 3-6). The broad selection of funds arose over the years to meet consumer demand for fund products that help meet a variety of financial objectives.

Professional Management

The money accumulated in a mutual fund is managed by professionals who decide on an investment strategy on behalf of the fund's shareholders. These professionals choose investments that best match the fund's objectives as described in its prospectus. Their investment decisions are typically based on extensive knowledge and research of market conditions and the financial performance of individual companies and specific securities. As economic conditions change, the fund may adjust the mix of its investments to adopt a more aggressive or a more defensive posture to meet its investment objective.

Diversification

Fund managers typically invest in a variety of securities, seeking portfolio diversification. A diversified portfolio helps reduce risk by offsetting losses from some securities with gains in others. Mutual funds provide an economical way for the average investor to obtain the same kind of professional money management and diversification of investments that is available to large institutions and wealthy investors.

MUTUAL FUND INVESTMENT OBJECTIVES

The Investment Company Institute classifies mutual funds into 33 investment objective categories.

EQUITY FUNDS

Capital Appreciation Funds seek capital appreciation; dividends are not a primary consideration.

- *Aggressive growth funds* invest primarily in common stocks of small, growth companies.
- *Growth funds* invest primarily in common stocks of well-established companies.
- *Sector funds* invest primarily in companies in related fields.

Total Return Funds seek a combination of current income and capital appreciation.

- *Growth-and-income funds* invest primarily in common stocks of established companies with the potential for growth and a consistent record of dividend payments.
- *Income-equity funds* invest primarily in equity securities of companies with a consistent record of dividend payments. They seek income more than capital appreciation.

World Equity Funds invest primarily in stocks of foreign companies.

- *Emerging market funds* invest primarily in companies based in developing regions of the world.
- *Global equity funds* invest primarily in equity securities traded worldwide, including those of U.S. companies.
- *International equity funds* invest primarily in equity securities of companies located outside the United States.
- *Regional equity funds* invest in companies based in a specific part of the world.

HYBRID FUNDS

Hybrid Funds may invest in a mix of equities, fixed-income securities, and derivative instruments.

- *Asset allocation funds* invest in various asset classes including, but not limited to, equities, fixed-income securities, and money market instruments. They seek high total return by maintaining precise weightings in asset classes. Global asset allocation funds invest in a mix of equity and debt securities issued worldwide.
- *Balanced funds* invest in a mix of equity securities and bonds with the three-part objective of conserving principal, providing income, and achieving long-term growth of both principal and income. These funds maintain target percentages in asset classes.

continued on page 4

continued from page 3

- *Flexible portfolio funds* invest in common stocks, bonds, other debt securities, and money market securities to provide high total return. These funds may invest up to 100 percent in any one type of security and may easily change weightings depending upon market conditions.

- *Income-mixed funds* invest in a variety of income-producing securities, including equities and fixed-income instruments. These funds seek a high level of current income without regard to capital appreciation.

TAXABLE BOND FUNDS

Corporate Bond Funds seek current income by investing in high-quality debt securities issued by U.S. corporations.

- *Corporate bond funds—general* invest two-thirds or more of their portfolios in U.S. corporate bonds with no explicit restrictions on average maturity.

- *Corporate bond funds—intermediate-term* invest two-thirds or more of their portfolios in U.S. corporate bonds with an average maturity of five to 10 years. These funds seek a high level of income with less price volatility than longer-term bond funds.

- *Corporate bond funds—short-term* invest two-thirds or more of their portfolios in U.S. corporate bonds with an average maturity of one to five years. These funds seek a high level of income with less price volatility than intermediate-term bond funds.

High-Yield Funds invest two-thirds or more of their portfolios in lower-rated U.S. corporate bonds (Baa or lower by Moody's and BBB or lower by Standard and Poor's rating services).

World Bond Funds invest in debt securities offered by foreign companies and governments. They seek the highest level of current income available worldwide.

- *Global bond funds—general* invest in worldwide debt securities with no stated average maturity or an average maturity of five years or more. These funds may invest up to 25 percent of assets in companies located in the United States.

- *Global bond funds—short-term* invest in debt securities worldwide with an average maturity of one to five years. These funds may invest up to 25 percent of assets in companies located in the United States.

- *Other world bond funds*, such as international bond and emerging market debt funds, invest in foreign government and corporate debt instruments. Two-thirds of an international bond fund's portfolio must be invested outside the United States. Emerging market debt funds invest primarily in debt from underdeveloped regions of the world.

Government Bond Funds invest in U.S. government bonds of varying maturities. They seek high current income.

- *Government bond funds—general* invest two-thirds or more of their portfolios in U.S. government securities of no stated average maturity. Securities utilized by investment managers may change with market conditions.

- *Government bond funds—intermediate-term* invest two-thirds or more of their portfolios in U.S. government securities with an average maturity of five to 10 years. Securities utilized by investment managers may change with market conditions.

- *Government bond funds—short-term* invest two-thirds or more of their portfolios in U.S. government securities with an average maturity of one to five years. Securities utilized by investment managers may change with market conditions.

- *Mortgage-backed funds* invest two-thirds or more of their portfolios in pooled mortgage-backed securities.

Strategic Income Funds invest in a combination of U.S. fixed-income securities to provide a high level of current income.

TAX-FREE BOND FUNDS

State Municipal Bond Funds invest primarily in municipal bonds issued by a particular state. These funds seek high after-tax income for residents of individual states.

- *State municipal bond funds—general* invest primarily in single-state municipal bonds with an average maturity of greater than five years or no specific stated maturity. The income from these funds is largely exempt from federal as well as state income tax for residents of the state.

- *State municipal bond funds—short-term* invest primarily in single-state municipal bonds with an average maturity of one to five years. The income of these funds is largely exempt from federal as well as state income tax for residents of the state.

National Municipal Bond Funds invest primarily in the bonds of various municipal issuers in the United States. These funds seek high current income free from federal tax.

- *National municipal bond funds—general* invest primarily in municipal bonds with an average maturity of more than five years or no specific stated maturity.

- *National municipal bond funds—short-term* invest primarily in municipal bonds with an average maturity of one to five years.

continued on page 6

continued from page 5

MONEY MARKET FUNDS

Taxable Money Market Funds invest in short-term, high-grade money market securities and must have average maturities of 90 days or less. These funds seek the highest level of income consistent with preservation of capital (i.e., maintaining a stable share price).

- *Taxable money market funds—government* invest primarily in U.S. Treasury obligations and other financial instruments issued or guaranteed by the U.S. government, its agencies, or its instrumentalities.

- *Taxable money market funds—nongovernment* invest primarily in a variety of money market instruments, including certificates of deposit from large banks, commercial paper, and bankers acceptances.

Tax-Exempt Money Market Funds invest in short-term municipal securities and must have average maturities of 90 days or less. These funds seek the highest level of income—free from federal and, in some cases, state and local taxes—consistent with preservation of capital.

- *National tax-exempt money market funds* invest in short-term securities of various U.S. municipal issuers.

- *State tax-exempt money market funds* invest primarily in short-term securities of municipal issuers in a single state to achieve the highest level of tax-free income for residents of that state.

Liquidity

Mutual funds are required by law to redeem shares on a daily basis, making mutual fund shares a very liquid investment.

Most mutual funds also continually offer new shares to investors. Many mutual fund companies allow shareholders to transfer money from one fund to another within the same fund family; these transactions are referred to as exchanges.

Mutual funds process sales, redemptions, and exchanges as a normal part of daily business activity. The volume of the transactions fluctuate over time depending on a variety of factors (see page 8).

The price per share at which shares are redeemed is known as the net asset value (NAV). NAV is the current market value of all the fund's assets, minus liabilities, divided by the total number of out-standing shares (see illustration below).

A fund's share price, or offering price, is its NAV per share plus any applicable front-end sales charge (the offering price of a fund without a sales charge would be the same as its NAV per share).

The NAV must reflect the current market value of the fund's securities, as long as market quotations for those securities are readily available. Other assets are priced at fair value, determined in good faith by a fund's board of directors. The Investment Company Act of 1940 requires "forward pricing": shareholders purchasing or redeeming shares receive the next computed share price following the fund's receipt of the transaction order.

How a Fund Determines Its Share Price

Mutual Fund X owns a portfolio of stocks worth $6 million dollars; its liabilities are $60,000; its shareholders own 500,000 shares.

$$\text{Fund Share Price or Net Asset Value (NAV)} = \frac{\text{Market Value in Dollars of a Fund's Securities Minus Its Liabilities } (\$6,000,000 - \$60,000)}{\text{Number of Investor Shares Outstanding } (500,000)} = \$11.88$$

Fund share prices appear in the financial pages of most major newspapers (see page 14). A fund's share price can also be found in its semiannual and annual reports.

Redemptions and New Sales of Long-Term Funds as a Percentage of Net Assets,* 1991-2000

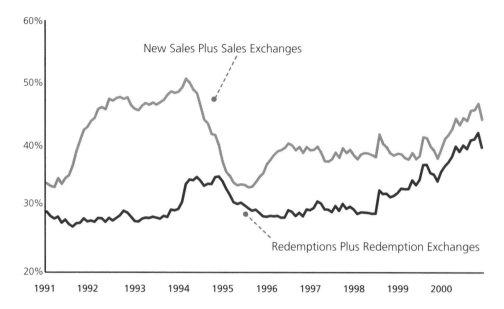

Redemptions and sales are represented as total new sales and redemptions, including exchanges, for running 12-month periods divided by average total net assets at the beginning and end of the 12-month periods.

Note: See page 105 for data points on this chart.

Any income and expenses (including any fees) must be accrued through the date the share price is calculated. Changes in holdings and in the number of shares must be reflected no later than the first calculation of the share price on the next business day.

Funds typically value exchange-traded securities using the closing prices from the exchange on which the securities are principally traded, even if the exchange closes before the fund's daily pricing time (which occurs with many foreign securities). If a material event that will likely affect the value of a security occurs after the exchange closed and before the fund's share price is determined, it may be necessary to determine the fair value of the security in light of that event.

Mutual Fund Minimum Investment Requirements, 2000

(percent distribution of funds by minimum investment requirement)*

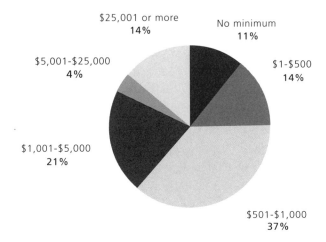

$25,001 or more
14%

No minimum
11%

$5,001-$25,000
4%

$1-$500
14%

$1,001-$5,000
21%

$501-$1,000
37%

*Many mutual funds offer lower investment minimums for Individual Retirement Accounts and automatic investment plans.

Note: Components do not sum to 100 percent due to rounding.

Pricing Process

Mutual fund pricing is an intensive process that takes place in a short time frame at the end of each business day. Generally, a fund's pricing process begins at the close of the New York Stock Exchange, normally 4:00 pm Eastern time. Fund accounting agents internally validate the prices received by subjecting them to various control procedures. For example, depending on the nature and extent of its holdings, a fund may use more than one pricing service to ensure accuracy.

Availability of Share Prices

The vast majority of mutual funds release their daily share prices through Nasdaq. For a fund's share price to be published in the next day's morning newspapers, it must be delivered by 5:50 pm Eastern time to Nasdaq. As prices are received by Nasdaq, they are instantaneously transmitted to wire services and other subscribers. Wire services transmit the prices to their client newspapers (see page 14).

In addition to newspapers, daily fund prices are available from other sources. Many funds offer toll-free telephone service, which provides the fund's share price and other current information.

Accessibility

Mutual fund shares are available through a variety of sources. Investors (outside retirement plans) may purchase fund shares either with the help of an investment professional (e.g., a broker, financial planner, bank representative, or insurance agent) or directly, based on the investor's own research and knowledge. Investment professionals provide services to investors—analyzing the client's financial needs and objectives and recommending appropriate funds. They are compensated for those services, generally through a sales commission or through 12b-1 and/or service fees deducted from the fund's assets.

Many mutual funds can be purchased directly from fund companies without the help of an investment professional. When funds are purchased in this manner, investors are required to do their own research to determine which funds meet their needs.

Mutual funds may also be offered as investment selections in 401(k) plans and other employee benefit plans. See Chapter 5 for more information on mutual funds and the retirement market.

Affordability

Shareholders benefit from competition in the mutual fund industry. Over the past 20 years, this competition has produced substantially lower costs and an array of innovative investment products and services.

Recent Institute research finds that between 1980 and 1998, the average "total shareholder cost" of equity mutual funds has decreased by 40 percent. The cost of bond funds and money market funds have dropped by 29 percent and 24 percent, respectively, over the same period. "Total shareholder cost" accounts for all major fees, expenses, and sales charges, and is based upon the same considerations underlying the fee information required by the U.S. Securities and Exchange Commission (SEC) in every mutual fund prospectus (see pages 12-13). Investors can easily discern all the fees a fund charges by looking at the standardized fee table. The table lists all fees charged by a fund and allows easy comparison of the costs of one fund versus another.

The fees and expenses mutual fund shareholders pay are subject to ongoing oversight and review by the fund's board of directors, including its independent directors. Directors have a responsibility under the law to protect the interests of shareholders (see pages 17-18). Fees are a major consideration when directors approve or renew the contract of a fund's investment adviser. Directors are responsible for ensuring that the level of fees paid by shareholders is reasonable and that shareholders receive value for the fees they pay. Directors also review and vote on fees and contracts with a fund's distributor, the custodian of the fund's assets, and other service providers.

Shareholder Services

Mutual funds offer a wide variety of services to shareholders. These services include toll-free telephone service, 24-hour telephone access to account information and transaction processing, consolidated account statements, shareholder cost basis (tax) information, exchanges between funds, automatic investments, checkwriting privileges on money market and some bond funds, automatic reinvestment of fund dividends, and automatic withdrawals. Mutual funds also provide extensive investor education and shareholder communications, including newsletters, brochures, retirement and other planning guides, and websites.

Shareholders Benefit from Economies of Scale

Recent studies by the U.S. Securities and Exchange Commission (SEC) and the General Accounting Office (GAO) confirm that mutual fund shareholders are benefiting from economies of scale. The SEC found that as stock and bond fund assets increase, automatic fee reductions in place at most mutual funds drive down expense ratios. Expense ratios for funds that have grown to more than $1 billion in assets, for example, are estimated to be nearly 50 percent lower than expense ratios for smaller funds that have yet to experience such growth. According to the SEC study, more than three-quarters of all fund shareholder assets are invested in these larger funds.

The GAO report confirmed that fees for equity funds generally declined in the 1990s. According to the GAO, 89 percent of the equity funds that experienced rapid growth in the past decade reduced the level of their annual fees, with the greatest growth typically leading to the sharpest reductions.

Both studies are consistent with ICI research that has found mutual fund operating expense ratios generally declining as assets grow and larger funds having lower expense ratios than smaller funds. The complete report is on the ICI website at www.ici.org/newsroom/industry_issues_fees.html.

Mutual Fund Fee Table Required by Federal Law

(example is hypothetical)

Maximum Sales Charge (Load) Imposed on Purchases

The maximum "front-end load" or sales charge that may be attached to the purchase of mutual fund shares. This fee compensates a financial professional for his or her services. By law, this charge may not exceed 8.5 percent of the investment, although most fund families charge less than the maximum.

Maximum Deferred Sales Charge (Load)

The maximum "back-end load" or sales charge that a fund may impose when shares are redeemed or sold; an alternative way to compensate financial professionals for their services. A common type of deferred sales charge is a "contingent deferred sales charge," which typically applies for the first few years of ownership, declining until it disappears.

Maximum Sales Charge (Load) on Reinvested Dividends

The maximum fee charged by a fund when dividends are reinvested in the purchase of additional shares. Most funds do not charge a fee for this service. Beginning in April 2000, new funds were prohibited from charging this fee.

Redemption Fee

Like a contingent deferred sales charge, this fee is another type of back-end charge when an investor redeems shares. Unlike contingent deferred sales charges, this fee is paid to the fund. It covers costs, other than sales costs, involved with a redemption. The fee is expressed as a dollar amount or as a percentage of the redemption price.

Exchange Fee

This fee may be charged when an investor transfers money from one fund to another within the same fund family.

Annual Account Maintenance Fee

This fee may be charged by some funds, for example, to maintain low-balance accounts.

Shareholder Fees are charged directly to an investor for a specific transaction, such as a purchase, redemption, or exchange.

Shareholder Fees

Maximum Sales Charge (Load) Imposed on Purchases	**4.5%**
Maximum Deferred Sales Charge (Load)	**None**
Maximum Sales Charge (Load) on Reinvested Dividends	**None**
Redemption Fee	**None**
Exchange Fee	**None**
Annual Account Maintenance Fee	**None**

Annual Fund Operating Expenses reflect the normal costs of operating a fund. Unlike transaction fees, these expenses are not charged directly to an investor but are deducted from fund assets before earnings are distributed to shareholders.

Annual Fund Operating Expenses

Management Fees	**0.75%**
Distribution (12b-1) Fees	**None**
Other Expenses	**0.22%**
Total Annual Fund Operating Expenses (Expense Ratio)	**0.97%**

Example

This example is intended to help an investor compare the cost of investing in different funds. The example assumes a $10,000 investment in the fund for one, three, five, and 10 years and then a redemption of all fund shares at the end of those periods. The example also assumes that an investment returns 5 percent each year and that the fund's operating expenses remain the same. Although actual costs may be higher or lower, based on these assumptions an investor's costs would be:

1 year	**$99**
3 years	**$309**
5 years	**$536**
10 years	**$1,190**

Management Fees

This is a fee charged by a fund's investment adviser for managing the fund's portfolio of securities and providing related services.

Distribution (12b-1) Fees

This fee, if charged, is deducted from fund assets to pay marketing and advertising expenses or, more commonly, to compensate sales professionals. By law, 12b-1 fees cannot exceed 1 percent of a fund's average net assets per year. The 12b-1 fee may include a service fee of up to 0.25 percent of average net assets per year to compensate sales professionals for providing services or maintaining shareholder accounts.

Other Expenses

These expenses include, for example, fees paid to a fund's transfer agent for providing fund shareholder services, such as toll-free phone communications, computerized account services, website services, recordkeeping, printing, and mailing.

Total Annual Fund Operating Expenses (Expense Ratio)

This represents the sum of all a fund's annual operating costs, expressed as a percentage of average net assets. Total annual fund operating expenses are also known as the fund's expense ratio.

Example of the effect of expenses on a $10,000 Investment

This is a hypothetical illustration required by the SEC in every fund's fee table. It is presented in a standardized format and based on specified assumptions (five percent annual return, expenses unchanged) in order to make it easier for investors to compare different funds' fees.

How to Read Newspaper Fund Quotes

The following is an example of how mutual fund tables appear in many newspapers.

The first column is the abbreviated fund's name. Several funds listed under a single heading indicate a family of funds.

The second column is the Net Asset Value (NAV) per share as of the close of the preceding business day. In some newspapers, the NAV is identified as the sell or bid price—the amount per share you would receive if you sold your shares (less the deferred sales charge, if any). Each mutual fund determines its net asset value every business day by dividing the market value of its total net assets, less liabilities, by the number of shares outstanding. On any given day, you can determine the value of your holdings by multiplying the NAV by the number of shares you own.

	NAV	Chg. NAV	Tot. Ret. YTD
Brlkd:			
Blgr Dfr	9.53	+0.01	+0.8
Bmo Pnc p	35.01	+0.03	+3.3
Bto Bmd	15.83	+0.13	-3.8
Cmyog			
MIA r	5.61	+0.01	+8.1
MIX	8.55	-0.03	+6.0
MIY t	14.90	-0.03	-7.7
MBF f	9.63	+0.07	-1.0
MBI	22.16	+0.67	+6.1
MBR	11.48	+0.03	+2.2

The third column is the change, if any, in net asset value from the preceding day's quotation—in other words, the change over the most recent one-day trading period. This fund, for example, gained $0.13 per share.

The fourth column is the fund's year-to-date (YTD) return expressed as a percentage of the NAV at the beginning of the year. The YTD return assumes the reinvestment of all distributions and subtracts annual expenses. The YTD return, however, does not reflect sales charges ("loads") or redemption fees. This fund, for example, gained 8.1 percent per share since the beginning of the year.

A "p" following the abbreviated name of the fund denotes a fund that charges an annual fee from assets for marketing and distribution costs, also known as a 12b-1 fee (named after the 1980 U.S. Securities and Exchange Commission rule that permits them).

If the fund name is followed by an "r," the fund has either a contingent deferred sales charge (CDSC) or a redemption fee. A CDSC is a charge if shares are sold within a certain period; a redemption charge is a fee applied whenever shares are sold.

A "t" designates a fund that has both a CDSC or a redemption fee and a 12b-1 fee.

An "f" indicates a fund that reports the previous day's prices, instead of the current day's.

Other footnotes may apply to a fund listing, and the meaning of footnotes may differ among newspapers. Please see the explanatory notes that accompany mutual fund tables in your newspaper.

CHAPTER 2

Regulation and Taxation of Mutual Funds

M utual funds are highly regulated financial entities that must comply with federal laws and regulations. In particular, the U.S. Securities and Exchange Commission (SEC) regulates mutual funds under the Investment Company Act of 1940. The 1940 Act imposes restrictions not only on mutual funds but also on their investment advisers, principal underwriters, directors, officers, and employees. The 1940 Act also regulates the two other types of investment companies—closed-end funds and unit investment trusts.

Four Principal Securities Laws Govern Mutual Funds

The Investment Company Act of 1940 regulates the structure and operations of mutual funds and other investment companies. Among other things, the 1940 Act requires mutual funds to maintain detailed books and records, safeguard their portfolio securities, and file semiannual reports with the U.S. Securities and Exchange Commission (SEC).

The Securities Act of 1933 requires federal registration of all public offerings of securities, including mutual fund shares. The 1933 Act also requires that all prospective investors receive a current prospectus describing the fund.

The Securities Exchange Act of 1934 regulates broker-dealers, including mutual fund principal underwriters and others who sell mutual fund shares, and requires them to register with the SEC. Among other things, the 1934 Act requires registered broker-dealers to maintain extensive books and records, segregate customer securities in adequate custodial accounts, and file detailed, annual financial reports with the SEC.

The Investment Advisers Act of 1940 requires federal registration of all investment advisers to mutual funds. The Advisers Act contains various antifraud provisions and requires fund advisers to meet recordkeeping, reporting, and other requirements.

Virtually all mutual funds are externally managed. They do not have employees of their own. Instead, their operations are conducted by affiliated organizations and independent contractors. The diagram on page 19 depicts the structure of a typical mutual fund, including its principal service providers

Shareholders

Like shareholders of other companies, mutual fund shareholders have specific voting rights. These include the right to elect directors at meetings called for that purpose (subject to a limited exception for filling vacancies). Also, material changes in the terms of a fund's investment advisory contract must be approved by a shareholder vote, and funds seeking to change investment objectives or policies deemed fundamental must seek shareholder approval.

Mutual Fund Disclosure—Informing Investors

To protect investors, all mutual funds are highly regulated by the federal government through the U.S. Securities and Exchange Commission (SEC). As part of this government regulation, all funds must provide two types of documents to investors free of charge: a prospectus and a shareholder report.

A mutual fund's prospectus describes the fund's goals, fees and expenses, investment strategies and risks, as well as information on how to buy and sell shares. A fund's current prospectus can be obtained from the fund, a broker, or financial planner. The SEC requires a fund to provide a full prospectus either before an investment or together with the confirmation statement of an initial investment.

Annual and semiannual shareholder reports discuss the fund's recent performance and include other important information, such as the fund's financial statements. By examining these reports, an investor can learn if a fund has been effective in meeting the goals and investment strategies described in the fund's prospectus.

Directors

A mutual fund is governed by a board of directors. The directors of a mutual fund are responsible for overseeing the management of the fund's business affairs. Because mutual fund directors are, in essence, looking out for shareholders' money, the law holds directors to a very high standard. They must exercise the care that a reasonably prudent person would take with his or her own business. They are expected to exercise sound business judgment, establish procedures, and undertake oversight and review of the performance of the investment adviser, principal underwriter, and others that perform services for the fund. Lawyers call this being a "fiduciary" or having a "fiduciary duty." This means a director is expected to obtain adequate information about items that come before the board and to exercise his or her "business judgment," a legal concept that involves a good-faith effort by the director.

According to new SEC rules, a majority of most funds' boards of directors must be independent of their fund's investment adviser or principal underwriter (see *SEC Enhances Independence of Fund Directors* on page 18). Independent fund directors serve as watchdogs for the shareholders' interests and oversee a fund's investment adviser and others closely affiliated with the fund.

Investment Advisers

An investment adviser is responsible for selecting portfolio investments consistent with the objectives and policies stated in the mutual fund's prospectus. The investment adviser places portfolio orders with broker-dealers and is responsible for obtaining the best overall execution of those orders.

A written contract between a mutual fund and its investment adviser specifies the services the adviser performs. Most advisory contracts provide that the adviser receive an annual fee based on a percentage of the fund's average net assets (see *Management Fees* on page 13).

The adviser is subject to numerous legal restrictions, especially regarding transactions between itself and the fund it advises.

Administrators

Administrative services may be provided to a fund by an affiliate of the fund, such as the investment adviser, or by an unaffiliated third party. Administrative services include overseeing the performance of other companies that provide services to the fund and ensuring that the fund's operations comply with legal requirements. Typically, a fund administrator pays for office costs and personnel, provides general accounting services, and may also prepare and file SEC, tax, shareholder, and other reports.

SEC Enhances Independence of Fund Directors

Mutual funds are the only companies in America that are required by law to have independent directors. This system of overseeing the interests of mutual fund shareholders has helped the industry avoid systemic problems and contributed significantly to public confidence in mutual funds.

The SEC has long recognized that independent directors play a critical role in the governance of mutual funds. In January 2001, the SEC adopted substantive rule and form amendments designed to enhance the independence of investment company directors and provide investors with more information to assess directors' independence.

The adopted amendments require, for funds relying on certain exemptive rules, that:

- independent directors constitute at least a majority of the fund's board of directors;
- independent directors select and nominate other independent directors; and
- any legal counsel for the fund's independent directors be an independent legal counsel.

In addition, the SEC requires funds to provide extensive information about directors, including:

- basic information about the identity and business experience of directors;
- fund shares owned by directors;
- information about directors that may raise conflict-of-interest concerns; and
- the board's role in governing the fund.

For a detailed discussion of the new fund governance rules, visit ICI's website at www.ici.org/issues/fund_governance.html.

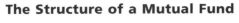

The Structure of a Mutual Fund

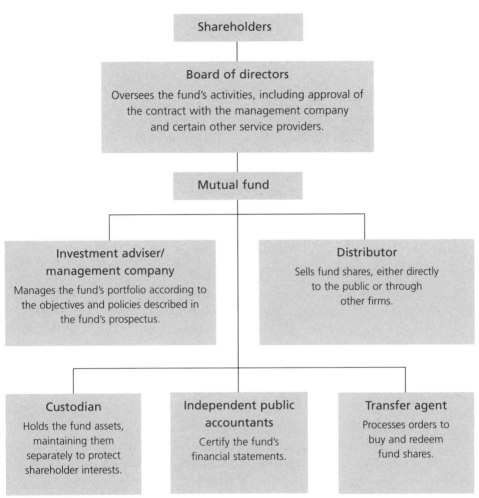

Shareholders

Board of directors
Oversees the fund's activities, including approval of the contract with the management company and certain other service providers.

Mutual fund

Investment adviser/ management company
Manages the fund's portfolio according to the objectives and policies described in the fund's prospectus.

Distributor
Sells fund shares, either directly to the public or through other firms.

Custodian
Holds the fund assets, maintaining them separately to protect shareholder interests.

Independent public accountants
Certify the fund's financial statements.

Transfer agent
Processes orders to buy and redeem fund shares.

Principal Underwriters

Most mutual funds continuously offer new shares to the public at a price based on the current value of fund assets plus any sales charges. Mutual funds usually distribute their shares through principal underwriters. Principal underwriters are regulated as broker-dealers and are subject to National Association of Securities Dealers, Inc. rules governing mutual fund sales practices.

Custodians

Mutual funds are required by law to protect their portfolio securities by placing them with a custodian. Nearly all mutual funds use qualified bank custodians. The SEC requires mutual fund custodians to segregate mutual fund portfolio securities from other bank assets.

Transfer Agents

A transfer agent is employed by a mutual fund to conduct recordkeeping and related functions. Transfer agents maintain records of shareholder accounts, calculate and disburse dividends, and prepare and mail shareholder account statements, federal income tax information, and other shareholder notices. Some transfer agents prepare and mail statements confirming shareholder transactions and account balances, and maintain customer service departments to respond to shareholder inquiries.

Taxation, Tax Exemption, and Tax Deferral

Unlike most corporations, a mutual fund generally distributes all of its earnings each year and is taxed only on amounts it retains. Thus, the fund's earnings typically are taxed only once—when received by the fund's shareholders.

This specialized "pass-through" tax treatment of mutual fund income and capital gains was established under the Revenue Act of 1936 and endures today under Subchapter M of the Internal Revenue Code of 1986. To qualify for this favorable tax treatment under the Code, mutual funds must meet, among other conditions, various investment diversification standards and pass a test regarding the source of their income.

Types of Distributions

Mutual funds make two types of taxable distributions to shareholders every year: ordinary dividends and capital gains. *Dividend distributions* come primarily from the interest and dividends earned by the securities in a fund's portfolio, after expenses are paid by the fund. These distributions must be reported as dividends on an investor's tax return. *Capital gain distributions* represent a fund's net gains, if any, from the sale of securities held in its portfolio for more than one year. When gains from these sales exceed losses, they are distributed to shareholders. Beginning in 2001, distributions of capital gains on assets held by the fund for more than five years will be eligible for treatment as "qualified five-year gains"—taxable at an 8 percent rate—instead of the traditional 10 percent rate for these gains.

At tax time, mutual funds send investors Form 1099-DIV, which tells them what earnings, if any, to report on their income tax return. Ordinary dividends are reported as dividend income; capital gain distributions and qualified five-year gain distributions (for eligible investors) are reported as such—regardless of how long the taxpayer has owned the fund shares.

Year-End Distributions from Mutual Funds

Investors often hear suggestions, around November and December, to postpone large, lump-sum mutual fund share purchases until January. Mutual funds some-times make large taxable distributions around this time, the argument goes, and an investor can avoid taxes by waiting the few weeks until the new tax year begins on January 1.

Several important factors—relating to the type of fund and the amount of any expected distribution—should be considered before pursuing such a "timing" strategy. First, the timing of investments in money market funds is irrelevant. These funds declare dividends daily and seek to maintain a $1 share price; investors incur a tax liability on the dividends declared each day. Second, funds that distribute their income more frequently (e.g., monthly or quarterly) make the timing issue less important. For example, bond funds usually offer periodic distributions, making year-end payouts typically small. Third, even for funds that distribute only once per year, the year-end payout may not be large. Funds with relatively low portfolio turnover, such as index funds, may have no capital gains to distribute.

Overall, the benefits of timed transactions may be outweighed by the market risks they entail. An increase in a share price while waiting to buy could cost more than the tax an investor is trying to avoid.

How Dividend and Capital Gain Distributions Affect a Fund's Share Price

Whenever funds distribute dividends and capital gains to share-holders, the share price or net asset value (NAV) drops by the amount distributed. For example, an investor buys 10 shares of a fund for $100 at an NAV of $10. Later, the fund distributes a capital gain of 50 cents per share and ordinary income of 50 cents per share (for a total of $1 per share). At that point, the shareholder receives a $10 dividend, the NAV drops to $9 a share, and the total value of the shareholder's 10 shares declines to $90.

Despite the lower post-distribution price, the total value of the shareholder's investment remains unchanged. If the shareholder reinvested the dividend, 1.1 additional shares (with an NAV of $9) are purchased for $10 and the total value of the 11.1 shares returns to $100. If the $10 is retained, the investor has 10 shares worth $90 and $10 in cash.

Share Sales and Exchanges

An investor who sells mutual fund shares usually incurs a capital gain or loss in the year the shares are sold; an exchange of shares between funds in the same fund family also results in either a capital gain or loss (see *Tax-Deferred Retirement Accounts* on page 25 for exceptions to these rules).

Investors are liable for tax on any capital gain arising from the sale of fund shares, just as they would be if they sold any other security such as a stock or bond. Capital losses from mutual fund share sales and exchanges, like capital losses from other investments, may be used to offset other gains in the current year and thereafter.

The amount of a shareholder's gain or loss on fund shares is determined by the difference between the "cost basis" of the shares (generally, the purchase price for shares, including those acquired with reinvested dividends) and the sale price. To figure the gain or loss on a sale of shares, it is essential to know the cost basis. Many funds provide cost basis information to shareholders or compute gains and losses for shares sold.

Capital Gain Distributions Paid by Mutual Funds
(billions of dollars)

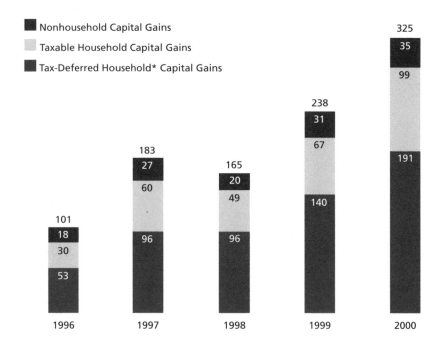

■ Nonhousehold Capital Gains
▫ Taxable Household Capital Gains
■ Tax-Deferred Household* Capital Gains

1996 — 101: 18, 30, 53
1997 — 183: 27, 60, 96
1998 — 165: 20, 49, 96
1999 — 238: 31, 67, 140
2000 — 325: 35, 99, 191

* Households are defined to exclude mutual fund assets attributed to business corporations, financial institutions, nonprofit organizations, other institutional investors, and fiduciaries.

Gains and losses on the sale or exchange of fund shares are reported on Part I of Schedule D on Form 1040 (*Short-Term Capital Gains and Losses*) if the shares were held for one year or less, and on Part II (*Long-Term Capital Gains and Losses*) if held for more than one year. Beginning in 2001, gains on the sale of shares held for more than five years would be reported (for certain shareholders) as qualified five-year gains.

After-Tax Returns

Mutual fund shareholders who have taxable accounts should understand the impact that taxes can have on the returns generated by their investments. In January 2001, the SEC adopted a rule that requires mutual funds to disclose standardized after-tax returns for one-, five-, and 10-year periods. After-tax returns, which will accompany before-tax returns in fund prospectuses, are presented in two ways:

- after taxes on fund distributions only (pre-liquidation); and
- after taxes on fund distributions and an assumed redemption of fund shares (post-liquidation).

While understanding the tax consequences of investing in mutual funds is important, shareholders must also be aware that assumptions in the after-tax return calculations may not reflect their current tax situation. For instance, after-tax returns are calculated using the highest individual federal income tax rate—a rate that applies to only a very small portion of fund shareholders. In addition, short-term capital gain rates are used in the one-year after-tax return calculation; however, holding shares for one more day would make them eligible for lower long-term capital gain rates.

Tax-Exempt Funds

Tax-exempt bond funds pay dividends earned from municipal bond interest. This income is exempt from federal income tax and, in some cases, state and local taxes as well. Tax-exempt money market funds invest in short-term municipal securities and also pay exempt-interest dividends.

Even though income from these two types of funds is generally tax-exempt, investors must report it on their income tax returns. Tax-exempt mutual funds provide investors with this information in a year-end statement, and they typically explain how to handle tax-exempt dividends on a state-by-state basis. For some taxpayers, portions of income earned by tax-exempt funds may also be subject to the federal alternative minimum tax.

Even though municipal bond dividends and interest may be tax-free, an investor who redeems tax-exempt fund shares may realize a taxable capital gain. An investor may also realize a taxable gain from a tax-exempt fund if the fund manager sells securities during the year for a net gain.

Tax-Deferred Retirement Accounts

Mutual fund investments in certain retirement accounts are tax-deductible and, generally, dividend and capital gain distributions remaining in the accounts accrue tax-deferred until distributed from the account.

In employer-sponsored 401(k) plans, for example, individuals typically contribute pre-tax dollars from their salary to an account in the plan. Similarly, IRA contributions may be tax-deductible, depending upon a person's eligibility to participate in an employer-sponsored retirement plan and their adjusted gross income.

Taxes on mutual fund earnings are deferred when they remain in 401(k) plans, IRAs, and other similar tax-deferred accounts, such as 403(b) accounts. Thus, no tax is incurred as a result of dividend and capital gain distributions, or from the sale of fund shares, until the investor takes distributions from the tax-deferred account.

Distributions are treated as income, which is subject to the investor's federal income tax rate at the time of distribution. (Nondeductible or after-tax contributions to these retirement accounts are not subject to taxation at distribution, and distributions from Roth IRAs also may not be subject to taxation at distribution.)

For most investors, distributions from tax-deferred accounts typically begin at or near retirement age, at which time the individual may be in a lower income tax bracket. Investors who receive proceeds from tax-deferred accounts prior to age 59½ may incur a tax penalty in addition to federal, state, and local income taxes.

CHAPTER 3

U.S. Mutual Fund Developments, 1990-2000

Mutual funds grew to be a more important part of the U.S. financial system during the 1990s than they had been in the prior decade. Assets held in U.S.-based mutual funds rose from slightly less than $1 trillion at the beginning of 1990 to just under $7 trillion by year-end 2000.

Assets of Mutual Funds, 1990-2000

(trillions of dollars)

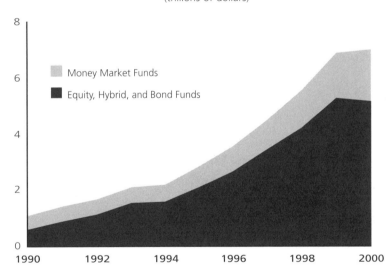

Note: See page 108 for data points on this chart.

A near-perfect set of economic conditions set the stage for the expansion of the mutual fund industry. Strong economic and corporate profit growth, low inflation, technological innovation, exceptional stock returns, and relatively low interest rates all favored securities investments, including mutual funds.

Asset Growth

Assets of U.S.-based mutual funds grew at an annual rate of 19.5 percent from the beginning of 1990 through the end of 2000. This growth has made mutual funds the largest financial intermediary in the United States.

Nearly half of the growth during the period was the result of fund performance—asset appreciation plus reinvested dividends and capital gain distributions—while 46 percent came from net new cash from investors, and the remainder was attributable to new funds.

Components of Mutual Fund Asset Growth,* 1990-2000
(trillions of dollars)

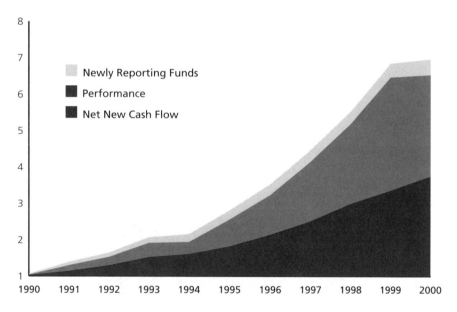

* Newly reporting funds are excluded from the calculation of fund performance and net new cash flow during the month in which they are introduced to the Institute's database. Asset levels plotted in the chart include year-end 1989 assets of $981 billion.

Note: See page 108 for data points on this chart.

Net New Cash Flow to Mutual Funds, 1990-2000
(billions of dollars)

	Equity	Hybrid	Bond	Money Market	Total*	Total Mutual Fund Assets
1990	12.9	1.5	6.8	23.2	44.4	1,065.2
1991	39.9	7.1	59.2	5.5	111.7	1,393.2
1992	79.0	21.8	70.9	(16.3)	155.4	1,642.5
1993	127.3	44.2	70.6	(14.1)	228.0	2,070.0
1994	114.5	23.1	(62.5)	8.8	83.9	2,155.4
1995	124.4	4.0	(6.1)	89.4	211.7	2,811.5
1996	217.0	12.3	2.8	89.4	321.4	3,526.3
1997	227.1	16.5	28.4	102.1	374.1	4,468.2
1998	157.0	10.2	74.6	235.3	477.1	5,525.2
1999	187.7	(12.4)	(5.5)	193.6	363.4	6,846.3
2000	309.6	(31.8)	(48.6)	159.6	388.9	6,965.2

Components may not sum to the total due to rounding.

Household Demand for Mutual Funds

As stocks and other financial assets earned relatively high returns in the 1990s, households shifted their asset allocations away from real estate and other tangible assets to financial assets. During this shift, households showed an increasing preference to invest through mutual funds rather than owning securities directly.

The number of U.S. households owning mutual funds more than doubled from 23.4 million at the beginning of the decade to 50.6 million in 2000. As a result, nearly one-half of U.S. households, representing 87.9 million shareholders, now own mutual funds.

Share of U.S. Household Bond, Equity, and Short-Term Assets*
Held Through Mutual Funds, 1990-2000

(percent of total)

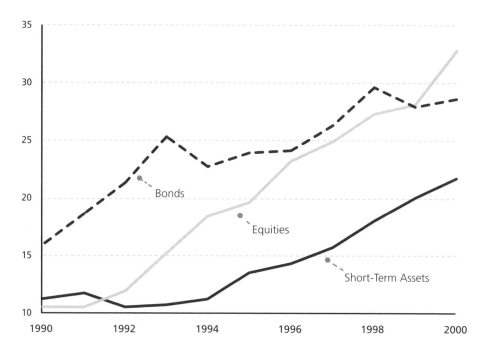

*Short-term assets consist of foreign deposits, checkable deposits, currency, time and savings deposits, and money market funds.

Source: Federal Reserve Board and Investment Company Institute

Note: See page 109 for data points on this chart.

Equity Funds. The share of household equity assets held in mutual funds reached 33 percent in 2000, up from 11 percent in 1990. Moreover, 85 percent of equity-owning households held a portion of their stocks through mutual funds in 1999, up from about 50 percent in 1992. Despite households' growing preference for funds during the 1990s, mutual funds hold only about 22 percent of all publicly traded U.S. stocks, with pension funds, insurance companies, and households' direct holdings accounting for the other 78 percent.

Mutual Fund Ownership of U.S. Corporate Equity, December 31, 2000

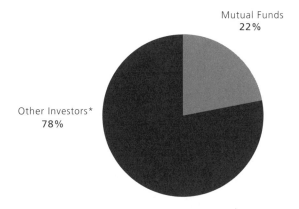

Mutual Funds
22%

Other Investors*
78%

Value of Publicly Held U.S. Equity Outstanding: $15.1 trillion

*Other investors include U.S. households, pension funds, and insurance companies.

Source: Investment Company Institute, Nasdaq, AMEX, and NYSE

Funds that invested mainly in U.S. securities (domestic equity funds) attracted 83 percent of the net new cash flow to equity funds during the 1990s. In 2000, net new cash flow to domestic equity funds was a record $260 billion, up from $176 billion in 1999.

World equity funds, which invest primarily in stocks of foreign companies, were also an important element of the growing mutual fund demand, as some investors increasingly sought to diversify their financial assets through overseas investments. Mutual funds are one of the primary vehicles many investors use to purchase foreign stocks, largely because of the difficulty and expense of making direct purchases of stocks not listed on U.S. exchanges. Annual net flows into world equity funds totaled $50 billion in 2000, up from $11 billion in 1999.

Net New Cash Flow to U.S. Equity Funds, Domestic vs. Foreign, 1990-2000

(billions of dollars)

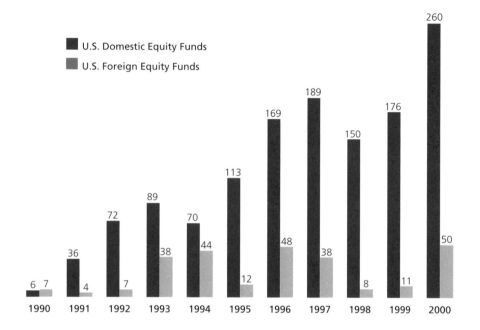

Note: The sum of the net flows to foreign and domestic funds may not equal the total shown on page 29 because of rounding. Data for funds that invest in other mutual funds were excluded from the series.

Bond and Hybrid Funds. Households increased their share of bond assets held through mutual funds from 16 percent in 1990 to 29 percent in 2000. Bond and hybrid fund returns were lifted by falling interest rates in the early 1990s, boosting inflows. During the second half of the decade, net flows to bond and hybrid funds were notably weaker and the shift toward indirect ownership of bonds slowed. Bond and hybrid funds experienced net outflows in 2000 as rising interest rates dampened household demand for these funds.

Interest Rate Spread and Net New Cash Flow to Retail Money Market Funds, 1991-2000

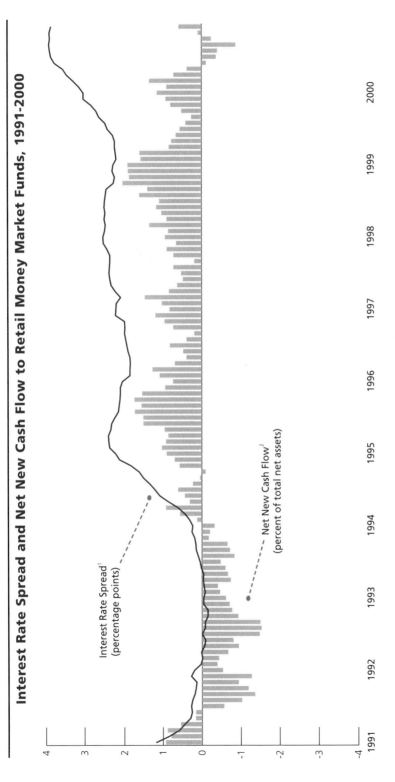

Interest Rate Spread[1]
(percentage points)

Net New Cash Flow[2]
(percent of total net assets)

[1] The interest rate spread is the difference between the taxable retail money market fund yield and the average interest rate on money market deposit accounts; the series is plotted as a six-month moving average.

[2] Net new cash flow is defined as a percent of retail money market fund assets and is shown as a six-month moving average.

Source: Investment Company Institute, Imoneynet.com, and Bank Rate Monitor

Note: See page 109 for data points on this chart.

Share of U.S. Business Short-Term Assets* Held Through Money Market Funds, 1990-2000

(percent of total)

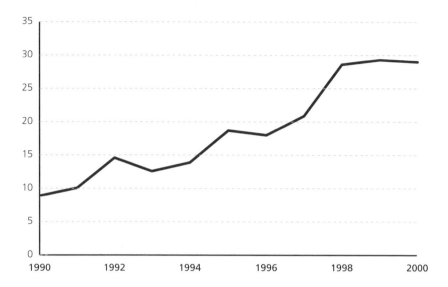

*Business short-term assets consist of foreign deposits, checkable deposits, money market funds, repurchase agreements, and commercial paper.

Source: Federal Reserve Board and Investment Company Institute

Note: See page 112 for data points on this chart.

Money Market Funds. The consistently higher yields of money market funds over savings deposits during the last half of the 1990s contributed to money market fund growth. After 1994, money market funds, on average, earned about 2.5 percent more per year than savings deposits. This wide yield spread encouraged retail investors to shift more of their short-term assets into money funds.

By the end of 2000, 22 percent of households' short-term assets were held in money funds, up from 11 percent in 1990. Between 1994 and 2000, the percentage of U.S. households owning money funds rose from 10 percent to 24 percent.

Net New Cash Flow to Money Market Funds, 1990-2000

(billions of dollars)

Retail

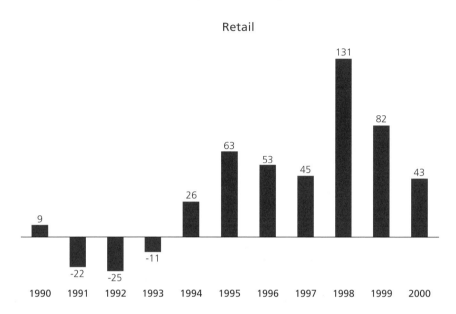

Institutional

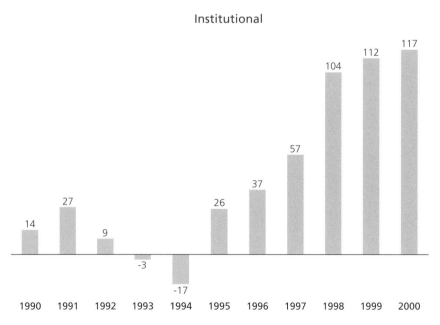

Institutional Demand for Money Market Mutual Funds

Businesses increasingly turned to money market funds for cash management during the 1990s. Money fund assets held by businesses (excluding financial services companies) grew at an annual rate of 24 percent between 1990 and 2000 from $26 billion to $219 billion. As a result of this growth, money funds' share of short-term business assets rose from 9 percent in 1990 to 29 percent in 2000.

The growth in business holdings of money market mutual funds is partly due to corporations' preference to outsource cash management to mutual funds rather than holding liquid securities directly. By using money funds, these corporations benefit from economies of scale provided by mutual funds that they would be unable to achieve through internal management of their liquid assets.

Other Industry Developments

The growing importance of defined contribution retirement plans, the development of new sales channels, a larger variety of funds, and lower costs also led to fund industry growth during the 1990s.

Retirement Market. With the growing popularity of defined contribution retirement plans, mutual funds expanded their presence in the private pension system. At the beginning of the decade, most retirement assets in mutual funds were held in IRAs. Employer-sponsored defined contribution plans became an important source of net new flow to mutual funds during the decade, either directly through plan contributions or indirectly from rollovers to IRAs. Plan sponsors increasingly chose mutual funds as plan investment options because funds provided more services than other types of pooled investment products and they satisfied regulatory criteria established for participant-directed plans. By year-end 2000, the shares of mutual fund assets in defined contribution plans and IRAs were roughly equal.

Share of Mutual Fund Assets in Retirement Accounts, Selected Years

(percent of total mutual fund assets)

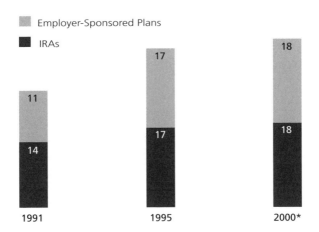

Employer-Sponsored Plans

IRAs

1991	1995	2000*
11	17	18
14	17	18

Preliminary data

Distribution Channels. With the rising demand for mutual funds in the 1990s, fund companies and distribution companies developed new outlets for selling mutual funds and expanded traditional sales channels. Overall, the estimated share of new long-term fund sales made directly to retail investors decreased from 23 percent in 1990 to 16 percent in 2000. Meanwhile, the new sales of long-term funds made to retail investors through third parties or to institutional investors rose from 77 percent to 84 percent.

Share of New Sales of Long-Term Funds by Distribution Channel, Selected Years

(percent)

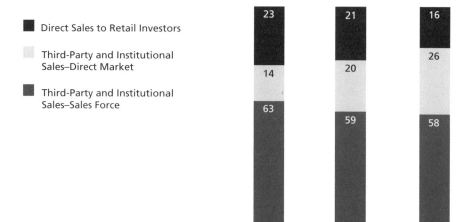

■ Direct Sales to Retail Investors

Third-Party and Institutional
Sales–Direct Market

■ Third-Party and Institutional
Sales–Sales Force

| 1990 | 1995 | 2000* |

Preliminary data

Many funds primarily marketed directly to investors turned increasingly to third parties and intermediaries for distribution. (Third-party distribution channels include employer-sponsored plans, mutual fund supermarkets, fee-based advisors, mutual fund wrap account programs, and bank trust departments.) For example, in 1990, an estimated 62 percent of new sales of direct-marketed funds were direct sales to retail investors, such as via mail, by telephone or the Internet, or at office locations; by year-end 2000, this share had fallen to 38 percent. Meanwhile, the share of new sales of direct-marketed funds conducted through third-parties or to institutional investors increased from 38 percent to 62 percent.

Likewise, funds that were traditionally sold through a sales force of brokers shifted increasingly to nontraditional sources of sales such as employered-sponsored pension plans, banks, and life insurance companies in the 1990s. By year-end 2000, the share of new sales of sales-force funds through nontraditional sources rose to 67 percent from 41 percent in 1990.

Size. The increased demand for mutual funds in the 1990s led to the creation of a large number of new mutual funds. The number of funds rose from around 2,900 at the beginning of the decade to about 8,200 by year-end 2000. Equity funds accounted for more than half of the new funds. Due to the rapid growth in the number of equity funds, the typical fund remained quite small. Half of the equity funds in early 1990 had less than $50 million in assets. Despite the enormous growth in overall equity fund assets, by 2000, median fund assets had risen to only $119 million.

The variety of equity funds also expanded, with fund complexes offering specialized funds appealing to diverse investor preferences. Also, domestic funds increasingly differentiated themselves by offering varied investment objectives, tailoring their investment portfolios according to market capitalization, sector, technology, and other attributes (see *Mutual Fund Investment Objectives* on pages 3-6).

Number of Mutual Funds, 1990-2000

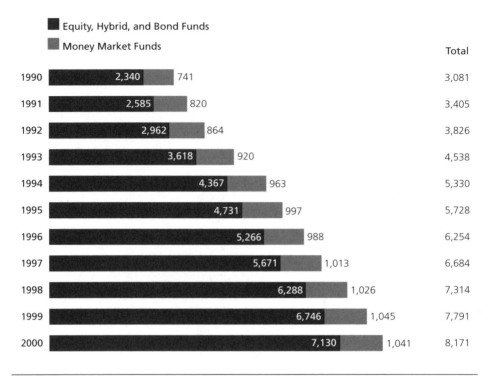

■ Equity, Hybrid, and Bond Funds
■ Money Market Funds

Year	Equity, Hybrid, and Bond Funds	Money Market Funds	Total
1990	2,340	741	3,081
1991	2,585	820	3,405
1992	2,962	864	3,826
1993	3,618	920	4,538
1994	4,367	963	5,330
1995	4,731	997	5,728
1996	5,266	988	6,254
1997	5,671	1,013	6,684
1998	6,288	1,026	7,314
1999	6,746	1,045	7,791
2000	7,130	1,041	8,171

Concentration. Although industry assets grew during the 1990s and many fund companies attracted substantial assets, asset concentration among the largest mutual fund complexes changed only marginally during the decade. The five largest fund organizations in 1990 held 37 percent of the industry's assets, whereas in 2000 the top five had 34 percent share.

Cost. Despite the increasing demand for mutual funds and the increasing number of services funds offered, the cost of owning mutual funds declined substantially across all major types of funds (see *Affordability* on page 10). From 1990 to 1998, total shareholder cost decreased by 25 percent for equity funds, 36 percent for bond funds, and 21 percent for money market funds. Since 1980, total shareholder cost has decreased by 40 percent for equity funds, 29 percent for bond funds, and 24 percent for money market funds.

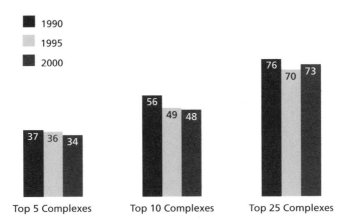

Share of Assets at Largest Mutual Fund Complexes, Selected Years

(percent of industry total)

- 1990
- 1995
- 2000

	1990	1995	2000
Top 5 Complexes	37	36	34
Top 10 Complexes	56	49	48
Top 25 Complexes	76	70	73

The decrease in shareholder cost likely reflected several factors, including increased competition among funds. Many load funds responded to competitive gains made by no-load funds by lowering distribution costs. In addition, many individual funds achieved economies of scale as their asset growth resulted in greater operating efficiencies. Consequently, many fund complexes were able to offer funds and fund services at a lower cost per dollar of shareholder assets.

Shareholder Behavior During Market Volatility

The broad, upward movement in U.S. equity prices in the 1990s was interrupted on several occasions by sharp but relatively brief market sell-offs. In addition, foreign stock markets suffered several periods of turmoil that sharply depressed returns on foreign-related stocks funds. The reaction of mutual fund shareholders to these periods of market volatility, however, was marked by restraint with no tendency toward mass redemptions.

Total Shareholder Cost for Mutual Funds,[1] 1990 and 1998

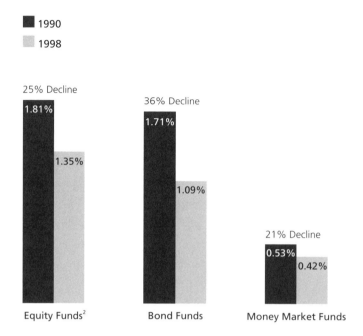

■ 1990
▢ 1998

25% Decline
1.81%
1.35%

36% Decline
1.71%
1.09%

21% Decline
0.53%
0.42%

Equity Funds[2]   Bond Funds   Money Market Funds

[1]Sales-weighted average of total shareholder costs for individual funds.

[2]Includes hybrid funds

Source: Investment Company Institute; Morningstar, Inc.; Lipper Analytical Services, Inc.; Value Line Publishing, Inc.; CDA/Wiesenberger Investment Companies Service; Wiesenberger Investment Companies Service; © CRSP University of Chicago, used with permission, all rights reserved (773.702.7467/www.crsp.com); Primary datasource & © Standard and Poor's Micropal, Inc. 1998 (617.451.1585/www.micropal.com); and Strategic Insight Mutual Fund Research and Consulting, LLC.

During U.S. market breaks in 1990, 1994, 1997, and 1998, domestic equity funds experienced net outflows that were small relative to assets and brief in duration. Net inflows typically resumed as stock prices recovered. Volatility in emerging markets in 1994, 1997, and 1998 also elicited a muted response from owners of international and emerging market funds.

This pattern of net flows is similar to the reaction of mutual fund owners during other market breaks since 1944, demonstrating a consistency in shareholder behavior that was not altered by the expansion of fund ownership during the 1990s.

CHAPTER 4

Mutual Fund Ownership and Shareholder Characteristics

An estimated 87.9 million individuals in 50.6 million U.S. households own the majority of the mutual fund industry's $6.965 trillion in assets. As of year-end 2000, they held $5.5 trillion, or 80 percent, of mutual fund assets, while fiduciaries—banks and individuals serving as trustees, guardians, or administrators—and other institutional investors held the remaining $1.4 trillion, or 20 percent.

Composition of Mutual Fund Ownership, 1990 and 2000

(percent of total mutual fund assets)

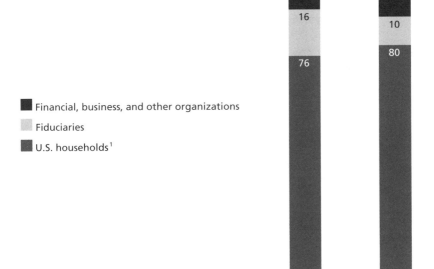

■ Financial, business, and other organizations

▨ Fiduciaries

■ U.S. households[1]

Note: Total assets of mutual funds were $1.065 trillion at year-end 1990 and $6.965 trillion at year-end 2000. Components may not add to 100 percent due to rounding.

[1]Household holdings include mutual funds held in retail accounts as well as through employer-sponsored pension plans, individual retirement accounts, and variable annuities.

[2]Preliminary data

U.S. Household Financial Assets

U.S. households own many financial assets, including mutual funds, stocks, bonds, and bank deposits. In 2000, households made $271 billion net purchases of financial assets, down from $476 billion in 1999. On balance, households were net sellers of directly held stocks and bonds but net buyers of mutual funds.

U.S. households invested $446 billion of their total net purchases of financial assets in mutual funds (including reinvested dividends) in 2000. Long-term mutual funds—equity, hybrid, and bond funds—accounted for $284 billion and money market funds, $162 billion.

U.S. Household Ownership of Mutual Funds, 1980-2000*
(percent of U.S. households)

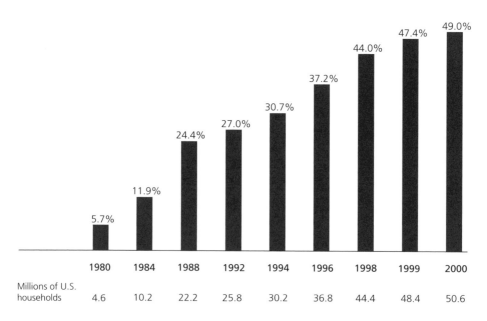

	1980	1984	1988	1992	1994	1996	1998	1999	2000
Millions of U.S. households	4.6	10.2	22.2	25.8	30.2	36.8	44.4	48.4	50.6

*U.S. households owning mutual funds in 1980 and 1984 were estimated from data on the number of accounts held by individual shareholders and the number of funds owned by fund-owning households; data for 1980 through 1992 exclude households owning mutual funds only through employer-sponsored retirement plans; data for 1994 through 2000 include households owning mutual funds only through employer-sponsored retirement plans. The data for 1998, 1999, and 2000 include fund ownership through variable annuities.

U.S. Shareholder Characteristics

The 87.9 million individuals who own mutual funds are, in many respects, a reflection of the U.S. population itself. Investment Company Institute (ICI) research finds that the typical mutual fund investor is middle-aged, married, and saving for retirement. More specifically, the typical fund investor is 44 years old, with median household financial assets of $80,000.

More than 80 percent of households with mutual fund holdings are headed by individuals in their primary income-earning years from age 25 to 64, with the heaviest concentration in the 35-to-44 age bracket. Only 17 percent of shareholders are retired from their primary occupation.

Most shareholders invest in funds for retirement, are willing to take at least moderate risk for moderate gain, and are not focused on short-term market fluctuations.

More than three-quarters of all mutual fund-owning households participate in an employer-sponsored defined contribution retirement plan. Sixty-two percent of fund-owning households own mutual funds in their defined contribution plans, and half view the work-place as their primary purchase channel for mutual funds. Fifty-seven percent have Individual Retirement Accounts.

The typical fund-owning household has $25,000 invested in mutual funds, representing nearly a third of household financial assets. Seven out of eight shareholder households include equity funds among their holdings. Eighty-two percent of mutual fund shareholders are employed full- or part-time. In married households, the spouse also tends to work. Half of all household fund owners made their first mutual fund purchase before 1990 and more than one-third did so between 1990 and 1995.

U.S. Mutual Fund Shareholder Characteristics[1]

Median

Age[2]	44 years
Household income	$55,000
Household financial assets[3]	$80,000
Household mutual fund assets	$25,000
Number of mutual funds owned	4

Percent

Household investment decisionmaker:	
Male is sole decisionmaker	24
Female is sole decisionmaker	22
Co-decisionmakers	54
Married or living with a partner[2]	74
Four-year college degree or more[2]	50
Employed[2]	82
Spouse or partner employed[4]	75
Own:[5]	
Equity funds	88
Bond funds	42
Hybrid funds	35
Money market funds	48
Have variable annuity invested in mutual funds	23
Own mutual funds bought:[5]	
Outside employer-sponsored retirement plan(s) (total)	54
Sales force[6]	39
Direct market[7]	25
Inside employer-sponsored retirement plan(s) (total)	62
Primary mutual fund purchase channel:	
Outside employer-sponsored retirement plan(s) (total)	50
Sales force[6]	34
Direct market[7]	16
Inside employer-sponsored retirement plan(s)	50

[1]As of 1998.

[2]Refers to the household's responding financial decisionmaker for mutual fund investments.

[3]Excludes primary residence but includes assets in employer-sponsored retirement plans.

[4]Percent of shareholders married or living with a partner.

[5]Multiple responses included.

[6]Includes funds purchased from full-service brokers, insurance agents, financial planners, and bank representatives.

[7]Includes funds purchased directly from fund companies and through discount brokers.

Note: Number of respondents varies. Data includes households owning mutual funds inside and outside employer-sponsored retirement plans.

Investment decisionmaking is shared in 54 percent of fund-owning households. Males are the sole decisionmakers in 24 percent of fund-owning households, females in 22 percent. Members of the Baby Boom Generation (individuals born between 1946 and 1964) make up the greatest percentage of mutual fund shareholders, at 51 percent. Twenty-seven percent of fund shareholders are members of the Silent Generation (born before 1946), and 22 percent are members of Generation X (born in 1965 or later). Thirty-one percent of mutual fund shareholders reside in the Midwest; 30 percent in the South; 21 percent in the West; and 18 percent in the Northeast.

Shareholders' Use of the Internet

The majority of mutual fund shareholders use the Internet, and nearly half of these online shareholders visit fund-related websites. ICI research finds that 68 percent of U.S. households owning mutual funds used the Internet between April 1999 and March 2000, up from 62 percent between July 1997 and August 1998.

Mutual Fund Shareholders' Use of the Internet, 2000*

(percent of U.S. households owning mutual funds)

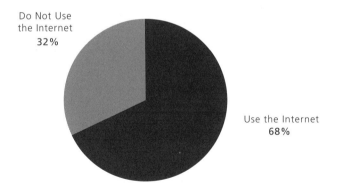

Do Not Use the Internet
32%

Use the Internet
68%

In the 12 months preceding the survey (April 1999 through March 2000). Excludes shareholders using the Internet only to send or receive e-mail.

The number of shareholders who visited websites offering fund shares (including mutual fund company and unaffiliated distributor websites) increased significantly, from one-third to nearly half, between the same periods. Shareholders who visited fund websites most frequently reviewed fund performance information, share prices, and personal account information.

Eighteen percent of all U.S. households that conducted mutual fund transactions between April 1999 and March 2000 bought or sold fund shares online. The median number of fund transactions conducted over the Internet during the 12-month period was four, while the average number was eight, indicating that a high volume of online transactions were conducted by a small number of shareholders.

Online shareholders were generally younger and had greater household income and financial assets than shareholders who did not use the Internet. The median age of online shareholders was 42, with a median household income of $63,900 and median household financial assets of $100,900. Online shareholders typically had $40,000 invested in four mutual funds and were college-educated. Shareholders who did not use the Internet were typically 51 years old with a median of $41,000 in household income and $84,000 in financial assets. These shareholders had a median of $32,500 invested in three mutual funds, and most did not have a college degree.

Use of the Internet to Conduct Mutual Fund Transactions, 2000

Mutual Fund Transaction Activity*

(percent of U.S. households owning mutual funds)

Method Used to Conduct Mutual Fund Transactions*

(percent of U.S. households owning mutual funds that conducted a mutual fund transaction)

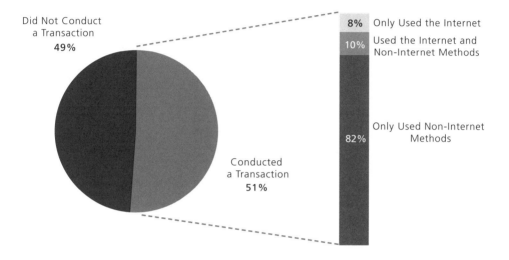

Did Not Conduct
a Transaction
49%

Conducted
a Transaction
51%

8% Only Used the Internet

10% Used the Internet and
Non-Internet Methods

82% Only Used Non-Internet
Methods

*In the 12 months preceding the survey (April 1999 through March 2000).

CHAPTER 5

Mutual Funds and the Retirement Market

Mutual funds accounted for $2.5 trillion, or 20 percent, of the $12.3 trillion U.S. retirement market at year-end 2000. The remaining $9.8 trillion of assets in the retirement market are managed by pension funds, insurance companies, banks, and brokerage firms.

U.S. Retirement Market Assets, 2000*
(trillions of dollars)

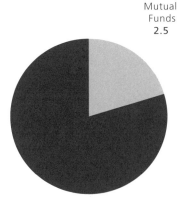

Mutual
Funds
2.5

Pension Funds,
Insurance Companies,
Banks, and
Brokerage Firms
9.8

*Preliminary data

Source: Investment Company Institute and Federal Reserve Board

Retirement Accounts Hold One-Third of Fund Industry Assets

The $2.5 trillion in mutual fund retirement plan assets represented 35 percent of all mutual fund assets at year-end 2000. Consistent with the slight decline in overall long-term mutual fund assets, which were pulled down by the weak equity market performance, mutual fund retirement plan assets edged down 2 percent during the year.

Mutual Fund Retirement Assets, 1991-2000[1]

(billions of dollars)

	Total Retirement	Employer-Sponsored Accounts[2]	IRAs
1991	336	147	189
1992	437	199	238
1993	608	285	323
1994	687	337	350
1995	941	464	477
1996	1,193	594	599
1997	1,542	774	767
1998	1,938	979	960
1999	2,510	1,266	1,243
2000[1]	2,453	1,221	1,232

[1]Preliminary data

[2]Includes private defined contribution plans (401(k),403(b), and others), state and local government employee retirement funds (and 457 plans), and private defined benefit plans.

Note: Components may not add to totals due to rounding.

Source: Investment Company Institute, Federal Reserve Board, Internal Revenue Service, and Department of Labor

Mutual fund retirement assets primarily come from two sources: employer-sponsored defined contribution plans and Individual Retirement Accounts (IRAs). Funds hold roughly the same amount of assets from each source.

Mutual Funds and the IRA Market

Assets in IRAs have continued to grow during the 1980s and 1990s despite the enactment of the Tax Reform Act of 1986, which limited the availability of tax-deductible contributions to IRAs. Asset growth has been primarily due to investment performance and rollovers from employer-sponsored plans. In addition, legislative changes in the late 1990s introduced new types of IRAs (SIMPLE, Roth, and Education).

Since the mid 1980s, the mutual fund industry's share of the IRA market has increased from 14 percent to 46 percent at year-end 2000. At the end of 2000, mutual funds accounted for $1.2 trillion of the estimated $2.7 trillion IRA market.

Assets in the IRA Market, 1990-2000[1]

(billions of dollars)

	Bank and Thrift Deposits[2]	Life Insurance Companies	Mutual Funds	Securities Held Directly Through Brokerage Accounts	Total IRA Assets
1990	266	53	141	176	636
1991	282	50	189	255	776
1992	275	56	238	298	866
1993	263	70	323	338	993
1994	255	79	350	372	1,056
1995	261	94	477	457	1,288
1996	258	110	599	499	1,467
1997	254	160	767	547	1,728
1998	249	190	960	752	2,150
1999	244	245	1,243	931e	2,663e
2000[1]	250	246e	1,232	922e	2,650e

[1]Preliminary data

[2]Bank and thrift deposits include Keogh deposits.

eEstimated

Note: Components may not add to totals due to rounding.

Source: Investment Company Institute, Federal Reserve Board, American Council of Life Insurers, and Internal Revenue Service

Mutual Funds and the Employer-Sponsored Pension Market

Mutual fund assets held in employer-sponsored retirement accounts totaled $1.2 trillion in 2000, a decrease of $45 billion, or 4 percent, from 1999. Mutual funds accounted for approximately 13 percent of the overall employer-sponsored market at year-end 2000. The employer-sponsored pension market is comprised of $2.1 trillion in assets in private defined benefit pension funds, $2.6 trillion in private defined contribution pension funds (and 457 plans), $3.1 trillion in state and local government employee retirement funds, $1.0 trillion in annuity reserves, and $0.7 trillion in federal government defined benefit plans.

Mutual Fund Assets by Type of Retirement Plan, 1991 and 2000*

(billions of dollars)

1991

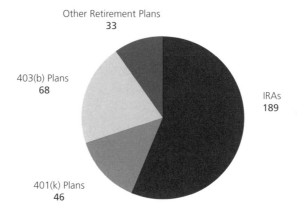

Other Retirement Plans
33

403(b) Plans
68

IRAs
189

401(k) Plans
46

2000*

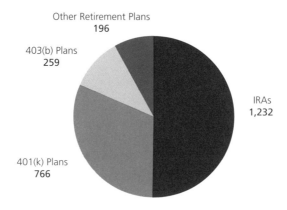

Other Retirement Plans
196

403(b) Plans
259

IRAs
1,232

401(k) Plans
766

*Preliminary data

Source: Investment Company Institute, Federal Reserve Board, Internal Revenue Service, and Department of Labor

Mutual Funds and the Defined Contribution Market

The most important source of fund assets in the employer-sponsored plan market is defined contribution plans, especially 401(k) plans. At year-end 2000, 65 percent, or $766 billion, of mutual fund defined contribution plan assets were held in 401(k) plans. Mutual funds' share of the 401(k) market has increased during the 1990s from 9 percent in 1990 to an estimated 45 percent at year-end 2000. Mutual fund assets in 403(b) plans were about 22 percent of mutual fund assets in defined contribution plans at year-end 2000, or $259 billion.

Assets in 401(k) Plans, 1990-2000*

(billions of dollars)

	Mutual Fund 401(k) Plan Assets	Other 401(k) Plan Assets	Total
1990	35	350	385
1991	46	394	440
1992	82	471	553
1993	140	476	616
1994	184	491	675
1995	266	598	864
1996	345	716	1,061
1997	466	798	1,264
1998	596	863[e]	1,459[e]
1999	780	935[e]	1,715[e]
2000*	766	946[e]	1,712[e]

*Preliminary data

[e]Estimated

Source: Investment Company Institute, Federal Reserve Board, and Department of Labor

401(k) Participants: Asset Allocations, Balances, and Loans

According to research by ICI and the Employee Benefit Research Institute (EBRI), 401(k) plan participants are making sensible investment decisions and accumulating substantial account balances.

Average Asset Allocation for All 401(k) Plan Balances, 1999

(percent)

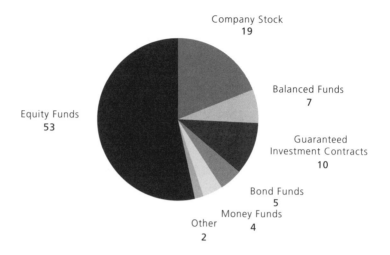

Note: Funds include mutual funds and other pooled investments.

Source: Tabulations from EBRI/ICI Participant-Directed Retirement Plan Data Collection Project

Younger participants tend to allocate a larger portion of their account balances to equity funds (which include equity mutual funds and other pooled equity investments), while older participants are more likely to invest in guaranteed investment contracts (GICs) and bond funds. For example, on average, individuals in their twenties invested 63 percent of their assets in equity funds, 4 percent in GICs, and 4 percent in bond funds. By comparison, individuals in their sixties invested 44 percent of their assets in equity funds, 19 percent in GICs, and 7 percent in bond funds.

The average 401(k) account balance, excluding plan loans, was $55,502 at year-end 1999, or 18 percent higher than the average account balance the year before. Workers in their sixties with at least 30 years of job tenure at their current employer had an average 401(k) account balance of $198,595.

Average 401(k) Account Balance by Age and Tenure, 1999

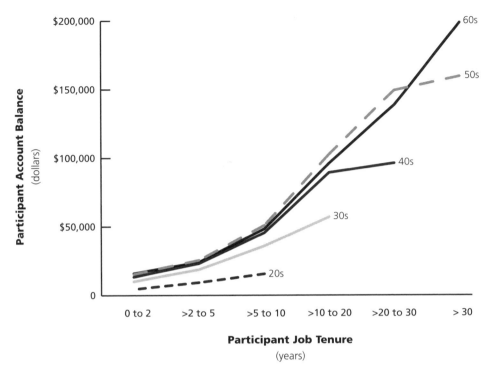

Source: Tabulations from EBRI/ICI Participant-Directed Retirement Plan Data Collection Project

Note: See page 113 for data points on this chart.

Most 401(k) participants do not borrow from their plans. At year-end 1999, only 18 percent of those eligible for loans had loans outstanding. The average unpaid loan balance for these participants represents about 14 percent of their account balances (net of the unpaid loan balances).

Types of Funds Used by Retirement Plan Investors

Of the $2.5 trillion in mutual fund retirement assets at year-end 2000, $1.9 trillion, or 76 percent, were invested in U.S. domestic or foreign equity funds. U.S. domestic equity funds alone comprise $1.6 trillion, or 67 percent, of mutual fund retirement assets. By comparison, only about 57 percent of overall fund industry assets—including retirement and nonretirement accounts—are invested in domestic and foreign equity funds.

Mutual Fund Retirement Assets by Type of Fund, 2000*

(billions of dollars)

	Equity		Bond	Hybrid	Money Market	Total
	Domestic	Foreign				
IRAs	$781	$123	$95	$92	$141	$1,232
401(k) Plans	537	69	36	71	53	766
403(b) Plans	211	16	7	11	13	259
Other Employer-Sponsored Plans	115	19	33	11	19	196
Total	$1,644	$227	$171	$186	$225	$2,453

*Preliminary data

Note: Components may not add to totals due to rounding

Approximately $396 billion, or 16 percent, of mutual fund retirement assets are invested in fixed-income funds: bond or money market funds. Bond funds hold $171 billion, or 7 percent, of mutual fund retirement assets, and money market funds account for $225 billion, or 9 percent.

The remaining $186 billion, or approximately 8 percent, of mutual fund retirement assets are held in hybrid funds, which invest in a mix of equity and fixed-income securities and derivative instruments.

About This Data Section

The data in the first five sections represent aggregate statistics reported to the ICI from individual mutual funds representing 95 percent of the U.S. industry's assets. Section Six provides data on open-end investment companies from around the world, and Section Seven features data on other U.S. investment companies besides mutual funds.

The U.S. fund data are classified according to two broad categories: long-term funds and short-term (or money market) funds. Long-term fund data are classified according to three broad fund categories—equity, bond, and hybrid—and further categorized into 29 more specific investment objective groupings. Short-term (or money market) funds are categorized into four taxable and tax-exempt investment objective groupings.

This Data Section begins with a breakdown of U.S. industry totals (pages 63 to 66), including information on fund assets, accounts, and the number of funds. U.S. industry totals are broken down from the short- and long-term categories into five separate ones: equity funds, hybrid funds, bond funds, taxable money market funds, and tax-exempt money market funds. The U.S. Industry Totals section does not provide total sales figures that combine long-term and short-term fund sales. Because of the special nature of short-term funds and their huge, continuous inflows and outflows of money, it would be misleading to add their sales figures to those of long-term funds.

Subsequent data sections on U.S. funds concentrate on:

- long-term fund statistics (pages 67 to 87),
- short-term fund statistics (pages 88 to 93),
- exchanges to and from all types of U.S. funds (pages 94 to 96) and,
- institutional investors in the U.S. industry (pages 97 to 99).

Table of Contents

Total Industry Net Assets, Number of Funds, Shareholder Accounts, and Complexes

Year	Total Net Assets (millions)	Number of Funds	Number of Shareholder Accounts (thousands)	Number of Complexes*
1970	$47,618.1	361	10,690.3	-
1971	55,045.3	392	10,901.0	-
1972	59,830.6	410	10,635.3	-
1973	46,518.5	421	10,330.9	-
1974	35,776.8	431	10,074.2	-
1975	45,874.4	426	9,876.1	-
1976	51,276.6	452	9,060.1	-
1977	48,936.9	477	8,692.6	-
1978	55,837.7	505	8,658.4	-
1979	94,511.3	524	9,790.0	119
1980	134,760.9	564	12,087.6	123
1981	241,365.4	665	17,499.0	134
1982	296,678.1	857	21,448.4	150
1983	292,985.1	1,026	24,604.7	164
1984	370,680.0	1,241	28,268.3	189
1985	495,385.1	1,527	34,762.3	217
1986	715,667.8	1,835	46,012.8	261
1987	769,171.9	2,312	54,421.2	314
1988	809,370.5	2,708	54,676.9	349
1989	980,671.1	2,900	58,135.0	357
1990	1,065,194.1	3,081	61,948.6	361
1991	1,393,189.3	3,405	68,334.8	361
1992	1,642,543.0	3,826	79,932.8	364
1993	2,070,023.5	4,538	93,217.3	375
1994	2,155,396.0	5,330	114,388.3	398
1995	2,811,484.0	5,728	131,231.1	401
1996	3,526,270.0	6,254	150,176.5	417
1997	4,468,200.6	6,684	170,521.1	424
1998	5,525,209.3	7,314	193,854.0	419
1999	6,846,339.2	7,791	226,872.9	433
2000	6,965,249.1	8,171	243,518.9	431

Note: The data contain a series break beginning in 1990. Data for funds that invest in other mutual funds were excluded from the series. Data prior to 1990 have been restated to create a consistent series back to 1984.

* A fund complex is a group of funds under substantially common management (or distributorship), composed of one or more families of funds.

Total Industry Net Assets
(billions of dollars)

Year	Equity Funds	Bond & Income Funds	Taxable Money Market Funds	Tax-Exempt Money Market Funds	Total
1970	$45.1	$2.5	–	–	$47.6
1971	51.6	3.4	–	–	55.0
1972	55.9	3.9	–	–	59.8
1973	43.0	3.5	–	–	46.5
1974	30.9	3.2	$1.7	–	35.8
1975	37.5	4.7	3.7	–	45.9
1976	39.2	8.4	3.7	–	51.3
1977	34.0	11.0	3.9	–	48.9
1978	32.7	12.3	10.9	–	55.9
1979	35.9	13.1	45.2	$0.3	94.5
1980	44.4	14.0	74.5	1.9	134.8
1981	41.2	14.0	181.9	4.3	241.4
1982	53.7	23.2	206.6	13.2	296.7
1983	77.0	36.6	162.5	16.8	292.9

	Equity Funds	Hybrid Funds	Bond Funds	Tax-Exempt Money Market Funds	Money Market Funds	Total
1984	83.1	7.8	46.2	209.7	23.8	370.7
1985	116.9	12.0	122.6	207.5	36.3	495.4
1986	161.4	18.8	243.3	228.3	63.8	715.7
1987	180.5	24.2	248.4	254.7	61.4	769.2
1988	194.7	21.1	255.7	272.3	65.7	809.4
1989	248.8	31.8	271.9	358.7	69.4	980.7
1990	239.5	36.1	291.3	414.7	83.6	1,065.2
1991	404.7	52.2	393.8	452.6	89.9	1,393.2
1992	514.1	78.0	504.2	451.4	94.8	1,642.5
1993	740.7	144.6	619.5	461.9	103.4	2,070.0
1994	852.8	164.5	527.2	500.6	110.4	2,155.4
1995	1,249.1	210.5	598.9	630.0	123.0	2,811.5
1996	1,726.1	252.9	645.4	762.0	139.8	3,526.3
1997	2,368.0	317.1	724.2	898.1	160.8	4,468.2
1998	2,978.2	364.7	830.6	1,163.2	188.5	5,525.2
1999	4,041.9	383.2	808.1	1,408.7	204.4	6,846.3
2000	3,962.3	349.7	808.0	1,607.2	238.1	6,965.2

Note: The data contain a series break beginning in 1990. All funds were reclassified in 1990 and a separate category was created for hybrid funds. At the same time, data for funds that invest in other mutual funds were excluded from the series. Data prior to 1990 have been restated to create a consistent series back to 1984.

Components may not sum to the total due to rounding.

Total Industry Shareholder Accounts
(millions)

Year	Equity Funds	Bond & Income Funds	Taxable Money Market Funds	Tax-Exempt Money Market Funds	Total
1978	6.8	1.4	0.5	-	8.7
1979	6.1	1.4	2.3	-	9.8
1980	5.8	1.5	4.8	-	12.1
1981	5.7	1.5	10.3	-	17.5
1982	6.2	2.0	13.1	0.1	21.4
1983	9.2	2.8	12.3	0.3	24.6

	Equity Funds	Hybrid Funds	Bond Funds	Taxable Money Market Funds	Tax-Exempt Money Market Funds	Total
1984	10.0	0.8	3.6	13.6	0.3	28.3
1985	11.5	1.5	6.9	14.4	0.5	34.8
1986	16.0	2.2	11.6	15.7	0.7	46.0
1987	20.8	2.9	13.1	16.8	0.8	54.4
1988	20.1	2.7	13.4	17.6	0.9	54.7
1989	20.8	2.8	13.3	20.2	1.1	58.1
1990	22.2	3.2	13.6	21.6	1.4	61.9
1991	25.6	3.6	15.5	21.9	1.7	68.3
1992	32.7	4.5	19.0	21.8	1.9	79.9
1993	42.3	6.8	20.5	21.6	2.0	93.2
1994	58.0	10.3	20.8	23.3	2.0	114.4
1995	69.3	10.9	20.8	27.9	2.3	131.2
1996	85.4	12.1	20.5	29.9	2.3	150.2
1997	101.8	12.9	20.2	33.0	2.7	170.5
1998	119.8	13.8	21.4	36.4	2.4	193.9
1999	148.3	14.3	20.7	41.2	2.4	226.9
2000	162.5	13.1	19.7	45.5	2.7	243.5

Note: The data contain a series break beginning in 1990. All funds were reclassified in 1990 and a separate category was created for hybrid funds. At the same time, data for funds that invest in other mutual funds were excluded from the series. Data prior to 1990 have been restated to create a consistent series back to 1984.

Components may not sum to the total due to rounding.

Total Number of Funds

Year	Equity Funds	Bond & Income Funds	Taxable Money Market Funds	Tax-Exempt Money Market Funds	Total
1978	294	150	61	-	505
1979	289	159	76	-	524
1980	288	170	96	10	564
1981	306	180	159	20	665
1982	340	199	281	37	857
1983	396	257	307	66	1,026

	Equity Funds	Hybrid Funds	Bond Funds	Taxable Money Market Funds	Tax-Exempt Money Market Funds	Total
1984	471	77	272	326	95	1,241
1985	579	87	404	346	111	1,527
1986	698	102	550	359	126	1,835
1987	843	146	782	388	153	2,312
1988	1,011	162	930	431	174	2,708
1989	1,069	175	992	463	201	2,900
1990	1,100	194	1,046	506	235	3,081
1991	1,192	213	1,180	553	267	3,405
1992	1,325	237	1,400	585	279	3,826
1993	1,587	285	1,746	628	292	4,538
1994	1,887	365	2,115	646	317	5,330
1995	2,140	414	2,177	674	323	5,728
1996	2,572	470	2,224	666	322	6,254
1997	2,951	501	2,219	682	331	6,684
1998	3,513	525	2,250	685	341	7,314
1999	3,952	533	2,261	702	343	7,791
2000	4,395	525	2,210	704	337	8,171

Note: The data contain a series break beginning in 1990. All funds were reclassified in 1990 and a separate category was created for hybrid funds. At the same time data for funds that invest in other mutual funds were excluded from the series. Data prior to 1990 have been restated to create a consistent series back to 1984.

An Overview:
Shareholder Accounts, Total Net Assets, and Liquid Assets
Equity, Hybrid, and Bond Funds

Year	Number of Reporting Funds	Number of Accounts (thousands)	Net Assets (billions of dollars)	Liquid Assets (billions of dollars)
1970	361	10,690.3	$47.6	$3.1
1971	392	10,901.0	55.0	2.6
1972	410	10,635.3	59.8	2.6
1973	421	10,330.9	46.5	3.4
1974	416	9,970.4	34.1	3.4
1975	390	9,667.3	42.2	3.2
1976	404	8,879.4	47.6	2.4
1977	427	8,515.1	45.0	3.3
1978	444	8,190.6	45.0	4.5
1979	446	7,482.2	49.0	4.7
1980	458	7,325.5	58.4	5.3
1981	486	7,175.5	55.2	5.3
1982	539	8,190.3	76.9	6.0
1983	653	12,065.0	113.6	8.3
1984	820	14,423.6	137.1	12.2
1985	1,070	19,827.7	251.6	20.6
1986	1,350	29,699.7	423.5	30.6
1987	1,771	36,746.4	453.1	37.9
1988	2,103	36,107.1	471.4	45.0
1989	2,236	36,820.8	552.6	44.6
1990	2,340	38,979.8	566.9	48.4
1991	2,585	44,778.8	850.7	60.4
1992	2,962	56,285.6	1,096.3	74.0
1993	3,618	69,632.0	1,504.7	99.4
1994	4,367	89,009.6	1,544.4	120.4
1995	4,731	101,094.3	2,058.5	141.8
1996	5,266	117,976.6	2,624.5	152.0
1997	5,671	134,897.0	3,409.3	198.8
1998	6,288	155,006.7	4,173.5	191.4
1999	6,746	183,257.3	5,233.2	219.1
2000	7,130	195,380.2	5,120.0	277.2

Note: Figures for shareholder accounts represent combined totals for member companies; duplications have not been eliminated. The data contain a series break beginning in 1990. Data for funds that invest in other mutual funds were excluded from the series. Data prior to 1990 have been restated to create a consistent series back to 1984.

Total Net Assets of Equity, Hybrid, and Bond Funds by Investment Objective

(millions of dollars)

	1998	1999	2000
Total Net Assets	**$4,173,531.1**	**$5,233,193.6**	**$5,119,954.0**
Aggressive Growth	394,175.3	623,855.6	667,719.5
Growth	890,077.5	1,286,616.7	1,250,888.0
Sector	120,742.2	204,588.1	235,127.7
World Equity–Emerging Markets	12,674.8	22,101.0	15,406.8
World Equity–Global	159,774.7	236,389.7	228,050.9
World Equity–International	187,185.6	276,226.8	262,136.1
World Equity–Regional	32,002.4	50,537.2	37,197.2
Growth and Income	1,032,842.7	1,202,141.2	1,137,450.3
Income Equity	148,751.4	139,433.8	128,320.0
Total Equity Funds	**$2,978,226.6**	**$4,041,890.1**	**$3,962,296.5**
Asset Allocation	40,113.6	39,004.4	36,621.6
Balanced	168,368.8	184,294.0	172,732.6
Flexible Portfolio	85,785.6	94,517.1	89,007.9
Income–Mixed	70,446.2	65,348.3	51,300.0
Total Hybrid Funds	**$364,714.2**	**$383,163.8**	**$349,662.1**
Corporate Bond–General	37,326.3	35,004.1	36,222.2
Corporate Bond–Intermediate-term	69,035.1	70,265.1	57,878.8
Corporate Bond–Short-term	37,147.6	37,761.7	35,774.7
High-yield Bond	117,443.5	116,904.5	90,374.8
World Bond–Global General	15,922.1	14,919.1	12,692.5
World Bond–Global Short-term	5,674.3	4,044.3	3,257.9
World Bond–Other	3,323.7	4,622.4	4,534.4
Government Bond–General	38,338.4	34,653.5	35,004.0
Government Bond–Intermediate-term	25,389.8	24,561.8	24,672.5
Government Bond–Short-term	19,735.0	19,599.6	17,139.9
Government Bond–Mortgage-backed	60,890.9	59,981.2	56,820.4
Strategic Income	101,769.1	114,188.5	155,696.7
State Municipal Bond–General	129,648.0	117,829.2	123,337.4
State Municipal Bond–Short-term	10,311.9	10,059.7	9,382.9
National Municipal Bond–General	126,756.0	112,448.7	120,517.1
National Municipal Bond–Short-term	31,878.6	31,296.3	24,689.2
Total Bond Funds	**$830,590.3**	**$808,139.7**	**$807,995.4**

Note: Data for funds that invest in other mutual funds were excluded from the series.

Liquid Assets of Equity, Hybrid, and Bond Funds by Investment Objective

(millions of dollars)

	1998	1999	2000
Total Liquid Assets	**$191,393.0**	**$219,097.9**	**$277,208.3**
Aggressive Growth	20,146.5	23,491.9	44,156.4
Growth	42,962.7	60,079.1	69,601.0
Sector	7,288.3	11,581.8	15,917.7
World Equity–Emerging Markets	949.6	651.1	947.2
World Equity–Global	11,224.0	14,790.8	21,732.5
World Equity–International	9,568.4	13,846.5	17,514.9
World Equity–Regional	1,061.9	1,754.4	1,372.6
Growth and Income	40,579.5	41,778.4	49,923.2
Income Equity	9,735.8	6,717.9	6,836.2
Total Equity Funds	**$143,516.7**	**$174,691.9**	**$228,001.7**
Asset Allocation	3,384.4	3,013.8	2,295.4
Balanced	7,707.3	7,667.3	8,192.6
Flexible Portfolio	7,869.6	7,525.4	9,258.6
Income–Mixed	6,607.7	3,063.6	4,386.1
Total Hybrid Funds	**$25,569.0**	**$21,270.1**	**$24,132.7**
Corporate Bond–General	558.0	840.2	941.5
Corporate Bond–Intermediate-term	755.0	1,920.6	1,192.3
Corporate Bond–Short-term	3,282.1	3,439.7	2,966.5
High-yield Bond	5,350.0	5,035.2	7,620.4
World Bond–Global General	908.2	1,022.2	497.3
World Bond–Global Short-term	458.3	312.6	276.6
World Bond–Other	147.3	281.6	130.7
Government Bond–General	(931.6)	(633.4)	383.1
Government Bond–Intermediate-term	482.8	472.5	1,079.3
Government Bond–Short-term	207.8	(684.9)	113.0
Government Bond–Mortgage-backed	(4,042.0)	(5,432.5)	(5,087.9)
Strategic Income	8,855.1	10,268.0	5,727.2
State Municipal Bond–General	2,179.8	2,402.4	3,703.4
State Municipal Bond–Short-term	217.7	316.0	432.8
National Municipal Bond–General	1,924.6	2,340.0	3,315.7
National Municipal Bond–Short-term	1,954.2	1,235.7	1,782.0
Total Bond Funds	**$22,307.3**	**$23,135.9**	**$25,073.9**

Note: Data for funds that invest in other mutual funds were excluded from the series.

Section Two: U.S. Industry Long-Term Funds

Liquid Asset Ratio—Equity Funds

Year	January	February	March	April	May	June	July	August	September	October	November	December
1970	7.6	7.5	7.3	7.9	8.8	9.9	10.3	9.8	9.0	8.6	7.9	6.6
1971	6.3	6.1	5.4	4.8	4.2	4.6	4.9	4.8	4.0	4.7	5.3	4.7
1972	4.7	5.1	4.7	4.1	3.9	4.4	4.8	4.9	5.0	5.5	5.0	4.2
1973	4.6	5.5	6.2	6.7	7.5	7.6	7.9	8.0	7.7	7.0	7.8	7.5
1974	8.0	8.4	8.6	8.9	9.1	9.3	9.8	10.9	11.8	10.7	10.7	10.1
1975	8.8	9.7	8.2	7.8	7.5	6.8	7.1	7.5	7.8	7.4	7.6	7.6
1976	6.0	5.5	5.1	4.8	5.2	4.8	4.6	4.7	4.5	4.5	5.0	4.9
1977	5.3	6.0	6.5	6.1	6.6	6.2	6.8	7.5	7.9	8.2	8.0	7.5
1978	8.5	10.2	10.3	10.1	9.5	9.2	8.0	6.9	6.5	6.7	7.9	8.2
1979	8.1	8.9	8.3	8.5	8.8	8.7	8.7	8.5	8.2	7.9	8.2	7.9
1980	8.5	9.0	9.2	9.5	10.4	10.1	10.4	10.3	9.8	9.7	9.3	9.1
1981	8.1	8.4	8.3	8.5	9.0	9.0	8.7	9.4	10.4	10.8	11.4	10.5
1982	10.5	10.4	10.8	10.5	11.4	12.2	11.0	10.1	9.2	8.9	8.4	8.6
1983	9.7	9.5	9.9	9.9	9.5	9.4	9.0	7.7	8.6	7.9	8.7	7.8
1984	8.0	8.5	9.1	9.4	9.3	9.7	10.1	9.5	9.3	8.8	9.1	9.2
1985	8.6	9.3	8.3	9.1	8.9	8.8	9.2	9.8	9.9	10.7	9.7	9.4
1986	9.6	8.6	9.1	9.9	9.5	9.2	9.8	9.6	10.1	9.7	9.5	9.6
1987	9.4	9.4	9.0	10.3	9.3	9.3	9.3	8.8	9.2	10.4	11.2	9.2
1988	10.1	9.9	10.3	10.8	10.5	10.1	10.6	10.6	10.6	10.0	9.7	9.4
1989	9.4	9.0	8.7	8.8	9.2	9.8	9.9	10.2	10.2	10.6	11.1	10.4
1990	11.5	11.6	11.9	12.5	11.3	10.7	10.7	11.9	12.8	12.9	12.4	11.4
1991	9.7	9.5	8.7	8.4	8.5	8.0	7.7	7.2	7.4	7.8	8.4	7.6
1992	7.1	7.2	7.8	8.3	8.1	8.7	8.8	9.1	8.5	8.6	8.8	8.3
1993	8.2	8.8	9.1	9.5	8.5	8.4	8.5	8.0	7.8	8.1	8.0	7.8
1994	8.2	8.6	7.8	8.0	8.4	8.3	8.6	8.3	8.2	8.3	8.9	8.3
1995	8.4	8.2	7.5	7.4	7.4	7.1	7.1	7.2	7.0	7.5	7.9	7.8
1996	8.1	7.4	7.0	7.0	6.6	6.5	7.0	7.1	6.7	6.3	6.3	6.2
1997	6.6	6.5	6.9	7.1	6.9	6.4	5.9	6.1	6.0	6.2	6.5	6.1
1998	6.4	5.7	5.2	4.8	4.9	5.2	5.2	6.0	6.3	5.9	5.5	4.8
1999	4.9	4.9	4.6	4.8	4.9	4.8	4.8	4.8	4.9	5.0	4.6	4.3
2000	4.4	4.4	4.0	4.9	5.2	4.8	5.0	4.7	5.3	5.9	6.5	5.8

Note: The data contain a series break beginning in 1990. All funds were reclassified in 1990 and a separate category was created for hybrid funds. At the same time, data for funds that invest in other mutual funds were excluded from the series.

Distribution of Mutual Fund Assets in Equity, Hybrid, and Bond Funds
(millions of dollars)

Year	Total Net Assets	Net Cash & Equivalent	Corporate Bonds	Preferred Stocks	Common Stocks	Municipal Bonds	Long-Term U.S. Gov't	Other
1985	$251,583	$20,598	$24,950	$3,771	$119,644	$38,322	$43,452	$846
1986	423,518	30,670	47,239	7,376	153,426	70,768	111,368	2,671
1987	453,081	37,942	41,591	5,557	176,076	68,463	119,653	3,799
1988	471,423	45,007	54,340	5,667	173,363	85,977	103,558	3,511
1989	552,585	44,676	52,823	4,571	240,749	84,820	117,835	7,111
1990	566,853	48,441	46,065	3,391	216,402	118,892	130,131	11,531
1991	850,748	60,386	86,931	6,606	375,007	149,533	163,284	9,001
1992	1,096,349	73,984	115,442	10,521	474,769	191,779	225,282	4,572
1993	1,504,705	99,437	165,595	16,209	696,083	249,163	272,264	5,954
1994	1,544,391	120,429	155,163	16,463	807,295	211,127	223,092	10,822
1995	2,058,466	141,761	190,890	16,914	1,198,422	245,331	259,117	6,031
1996	2,624,463	152,025	238,046	21,168	1,697,236	245,183	265,177	5,628
1997	3,409,315	198,826	292,616	29,529	2,328,723	266,310	282,377	10,934
1998	4,173,531	191,393	389,047	25,709	2,978,590	292,505	286,514	9,773
1999	5,233,194	219,098	387,809	30,909	4,028,638	267,434	294,104	5,202
2000	5,119,954	277,208	349,343	28,719	3,882,029	268,968	309,446	4,241

Note: The data contain a series break beginning in 1990. Data for funds that invest in other mutual funds were excluded from the series. Data prior to 1990 have been restated to create a consistent series back to 1985.

Net New Cash Flow* by Investment Objective
(millions of dollars)

	1998	1999	2000
Total Net New Cash Flow	**$241,796.1**	**$169,779.9**	**$229,204.9**
Aggressive Growth	$11,663.9	$34,340.2	$129,327.1
Growth	64,255.1	97,001.6	119,079.2
Sector	6,829.4	28,948.4	62,310.6
World Equity–Emerging Markets	98.9	763.9	108.5
World Equity–Global	4,297.5	3,091.2	22,716.6
World Equity–International	831.0	5,986.8	31,523.1
World Equity–Regional	2,299.6	1,382.5	(4,439.1)
Growth and Income	61,893.5	30,660.5	(31,981.6)
Income Equity	4,863.5	(14,509.4)	(19,056.3)
Total Equity Funds	**$157,032.4**	**$187,665.7**	**$309,588.1**
Asset Allocation	($4,184.3)	($5,236.5)	($3,002.5)
Balanced	8,077.9	(140.2)	(12,238.6)
Flexible Portfolio	2,618.6	(2,387.3)	(7,181.9)
Income–Mixed	3,641.9	(4,587.9)	(9,361.1)
Total Hybrid Funds	**$10,154.1**	**($12,351.9)**	**($31,784.1)**
Corporate Bond–General	$5,745.4	($505.3)	($586.3)
Corporate Bond–Intermediate-term	10,198.1	3,991.2	(2,109.3)
Corporate Bond–Short-term	4,177.5	733.7	(1,245.7)
High-yield Bond	13,601.7	(2,545.9)	(12,232.8)
World Bond–Global General	(1,306.2)	(1,423.0)	(869.8)
World Bond–Global Short-term	(171.4)	(559.2)	(609.2)
World Bond–Other	321.8	(388.5)	(870.8)
Government Bond–General	1,152.3	(2,620.0)	(3,283.5)
Government Bond–Intermediate-term	2,352.2	846.2	(2,293.8)
Government Bond–Short-term	2,841.2	(392.8)	(3,457.7)
Government Bond–Mortgage-backed	2,553.0	191.5	(7,321.9)
Strategic Income	17,944.7	9,295.1	437.7
State Municipal Bond–General	6,765.0	(4,602.4)	(5,740.5)
State Municipal Bond–Short-term	1,234.1	19.5	227.8
National Municipal Bond–General	4,177.4	(7,009.8)	(8,564.0)
National Municipal Bond–Short-term	3,022.8	(564.2)	(79.3)
Total Bond Funds	**$74,609.6**	**($5,533.9)**	**($48,599.1)**

Note: Data for funds that invest in other mutual funds were excluded from the series.

*Net new cash flow is the dollar value of new sales minus redemptions, combined with net exchanges.

Net New Cash Flow* and Total Net Assets of Equity Funds

(millions of dollars)

	Net New Cash Flow	Total Net Assets
1998		
January	$14,089.1	$2,392,569.3
February	24,060.8	2,586,483.9
March	22,437.6	2,733,526.9
April	26,191.0	2,792,090.0
May	18,847.8	2,750,361.9
June	18,991.9	2,835,775.5
July	19,341.8	2,806,322.9
August	(11,578.2)	2,359,355.7
September	6,254.8	2,479,182.2
October	2,378.3	2,646,860.9
November	12,821.9	2,813,423.8
December	3,195.6	2,978,226.6
Total	**$157,032.4**	**$2,978,226.6**
1999		
January	$17,221.8	$3,073,611.9
February	767.1	2,976,057.7
March	12,570.4	3,109,136.5
April	25,849.5	3,265,041.1
May	14,953.8	3,220,462.4
June	18,870.3	3,424,674.2
July	12,335.1	3,367,283.3
August	9,475.2	3,342,455.2
September	11,246.5	3,301,188.3
October	20,964.6	3,506,880.2
November	18,526.8	3,672,348.4
December	24,884.6	4,041,890.1
Total	**$187,665.7**	**$4,041,890.1**
2000		
January	$44,541.0	$3,956,475.2
February	55,616.7	4,231,193.9
March	40,220.3	4,441,463.1
April	35,521.5	4,246,897.4
May	17,254.2	4,106,534.5
June	21,962.8	4,320,183.1
July	16,762.5	4,246,366.9
August	24,139.4	4,571,767.0
September	17,594.6	4,388,756.8
October	19,322.1	4,283,996.6
November	5,048.5	3,854,878.6
December	11,604.5	3,962,296.5
Total	**$309,588.1**	**$3,962,296.5**

Note: Data for funds that invest in other mutual funds were excluded from the series.

*Net new cash flow is the dollar value of new sales minus redemptions, combined with net exchanges.

Net New Cash Flow* and Total Net Assets of Hybrid Funds
(millions of dollars)

	Net New Cash Flow	Total Net Assets
1998		
January	$2,555.1	$322,207.9
February	2,031.9	336,637.1
March	1,736.7	348,350.0
April	1,011.3	351,738.2
May	1,079.4	349,746.3
June	1,028.1	356,698.0
July	1,042.1	355,125.3
August	(948.5)	321,274.9
September	(518.2)	332,306.0
October	(208.8)	343,891.4
November	1,475.0	357,419.2
December	(130.0)	364,714.2
Total	**$10,154.1**	**$364,714.2**
1999		
January	$597.2	$368,855.5
February	(1,021.8)	360,534.6
March	(1,052.5)	366,758.0
April	(247.7)	380,762.3
May	(220.2)	374,697.8
June	(413.5)	384,464.5
July	(249.1)	377,594.6
August	(854.8)	372,966.3
September	(1,051.8)	366,714.0
October	(813.2)	375,011.1
November	(2,563.4)	376,779.5
December	(4,461.1)	383,163.8
Total	**($12,351.9)**	**$383,163.8**
2000		
January	($6,177.3)	$355,377.7
February	(5,136.9)	346,494.4
March	(5,698.1)	357,736.0
April	(1,938.4)	350,532.7
May	(2,089.3)	348,107.3
June	(2,238.9)	351,464.7
July	(1,666.2)	352,851.7
August	(1,605.8)	362,974.8
September	(2,165.0)	354,855.7
October	(1,178.6)	353,896.5
November	(263.1)	342,850.0
December	(1,626.5)	349,662.1
Total	**($31,784.1)**	**$349,662.1**

Note: Data for funds that invest in other mutual funds were excluded from the series.

*Net new cash flow is the dollar value of new sales minus redemptions, combined with net exchanges.

Net New Cash Flow* and Total Net Assets of Bond Funds
(millions of dollars)

	Net New Cash Flow	Total Net Assets
1998		
January	$9,102.1	$741,639.4
February	6,323.6	749,512.3
March	6,425.9	758,718.6
April	4,220.1	762,945.5
May	8,754.0	777,085.1
June	4,136.9	784,849.6
July	6,822.8	792,635.9
August	5,879.9	795,774.3
September	5,634.2	811,490.0
October	5,272.4	810,201.0
November	8,692.2	828,125.7
December	3,345.5	830,590.3
Total	**$74,609.6**	**$830,590.3**
1999		
January	$8,330.3	$843,956.2
February	4,380.2	841,827.6
March	6,232.6	852,026.9
April	1,651.4	859,105.5
May	(1,939.5)	847,738.0
June	1,857.1	841,913.1
July	494.9	839,924.4
August	(1,007.9)	833,062.5
September	(3,829.9)	830,490.8
October	(3,514.0)	823,189.0
November	(4,649.3)	823,651.8
December	(13,539.8)	808,139.7
Total	**($5,533.9)**	**$808,139.7**
2000		
January	($12,809.1)	$802,472.8
February	(8,155.2)	804,580.7
March	(7,680.3)	801,638.6
April	(6,714.1)	788,999.7
May	(5,086.4)	777,309.3
June	442.8	792,100.2
July	(238.7)	796,895.6
August	(1,859.3)	802,418.2
September	(3,120.6)	797,817.4
October	(2,019.0)	795,379.6
November	(633.0)	795,130.5
December	(726.2)	807,995.4
Total	**($48,599.1)**	**$807,995.4**

Note: Data for funds that invest in other mutual funds were excluded from the series.

*Net new cash flow is the dollar value of new sales minus redemptions, combined with net exchanges.

An Overview: Sales, Redemptions, and Net Sales of Equity, Hybrid, and Bond Funds

(millions of dollars)

Year	Sales	Redemptions	Net Sales
1970	$4,625.8	$2,987.6	$1,638.2
1971	5,147.2	4,750.2	397.0
1972	4,892.5	6,562.9	(1,670.4)
1973	4,359.3	5,651.1	(1,291.8)
1974	3,091.5	3,380.9	(289.4)
1975	3,307.2	3,686.3	(379.1)
1976	4,360.5	6,801.2	(2,440.7)
1977	6,399.6	6,026.0	373.6
1978	6,705.3	7,232.4	(527.1)
1979	6,826.1	8,005.0	(1,178.9)
1980	9,993.7	8,200.0	1,793.7
1981	9,710.4	7,470.4	2,240.0
1982	15,738.3	7,571.8	8,166.5
1983	40,325.1	14,677.6	25,647.5
1984	45,857.0	20,030.4	25,826.6
1985	114,233.0	33,761.9	80,471.1
1986	215,288.2	66,970.0	148,318.2
1987	190,207.2	116,060.6	74,146.6
1988	95,115.7	92,326.9	2,788.8
1989	125,339.0	91,526.5	33,812.5
1990	149,094.6	98,071.3	51,023.3
1991	236,342.3	116,584.2	119,758.1
1992	363,163.3	165,308.3	197,855.0
1993	509,916.6	230,983.9	278,932.7
1994	472,439.5	329,232.2	143,207.3
1995	475,526.9	312,936.7	162,590.2
1996	681,142.7	397,550.2	283,592.5
1997	869,025.9	541,192.6	327,833.3
1998	1,057,820.8	747,680.4	310,140.4
1999	1,273,620.9	1,021,188.8	252,432.1
2000	1,631,476.4	1,334,283.9	297,192.5

Note: The data contain a series break beginning in 1990. Data for funds that invest in other mutual funds were excluded from the series. Data prior to 1990 have been restated to create a consistent series back to 1984.

Sales of Equity, Hybrid, and Bond Funds
by Investment Objective
(millions of dollars)

	1998	1999	2000
Total Sales	**$1,057,820.8**	**$1,273,620.9**	**$1,631,476.4**
Aggressive Growth	$113,817.1	$153,230.4	$290,298.3
Growth	204,846.4	294,832.0	365,387.1
Sector	32,759.3	62,648.9	121,563.3
World Equity–Emerging Markets	7,511.7	7,308.1	11,628.1
World Equity–Global	39,723.4	47,807.3	85,584.2
World Equity–International	71,644.7	108,132.8	210,938.4
World Equity–Regional	18,096.2	22,786.6	27,060.6
Growth and Income	205,656.2	227,631.8	214,467.4
Income Equity	27,995.9	21,634.5	20,478.9
Total Equity Funds	**$722,050.9**	**$946,012.4**	**$1,347,406.3**
Asset Allocation	$7,199.5	$6,494.3	$6,688.2
Balanced	37,728.0	42,799.9	39,998.7
Flexible Portfolio	16,240.9	17,639.2	13,714.5
Income–Mixed	17,093.0	14,486.3	8,222.6
Total Hybrid Funds	**$78,261.4**	**$81,419.7**	**$68,624.0**
Corporate Bond–General	$14,377.1	$10,339.3	$11,235.0
Corporate Bond–Intermediate-term	24,936.7	24,907.3	16,857.3
Corporate Bond–Short-term	18,830.4	17,733.1	19,276.0
High-yield Bond	48,033.4	39,171.9	29,403.7
World Bond–Global General	4,457.0	3,495.0	3,724.6
World Bond–Global Short-term	1,931.8	1,576.7	1,367.6
World Bond–Other	2,029.8	1,911.4	2,017.8
Government Bond–General	10,948.2	10,536.6	9,043.1
Government Bond–Intermediate-term	8,032.8	8,895.3	6,385.5
Government Bond–Short-term	10,212.4	9,425.7	6,968.5
Government Bond–Mortgage-backed	14,403.2	15,368.1	9,854.4
Strategic Income	37,318.6	44,406.5	50,876.6
State Municipal Bond–General	25,620.2	23,319.0	17,803.2
State Municipal Bond–Short-term	3,123.6	3,104.7	2,607.9
National Municipal Bond–General	22,926.0	20,628.5	18,347.9
National Municipal Bond–Short-term	10,327.3	11,369.7	9,677.0
Total Bond Funds	**$257,508.5**	**$246,188.8**	**$215,446.1**

Note: Data for funds that invest in other mutual funds were excluded from the series.

Reinvested Dividends of Equity, Hybrid, and Bond Funds by Investment Objective

(millions of dollars)

	1998	1999	2000
Total Reinvested Dividends	**$60,038.8**	**$69,972.6**	**$67,093.5**
Aggressive Growth	$1,295.1	$1,828.2	$1,448.6
Growth	3,931.4	6,451.3	4,935.4
Sector	1,101.2	1,413.2	1,427.5
World Equity–Emerging Markets	156.6	86.1	110.6
World Equity–Global	1,285.4	1,732.3	1,835.7
World Equity–International	2,430.5	2,248.0	2,705.2
World Equity–Regional	356.4	298.8	247.9
Growth and Income	9,759.5	10,739.4	10,683.7
Income Equity	2,065.5	2,534.7	2,006.8
Total Equity Funds	**$22,381.6**	**$27,332.0**	**$25,401.4**
Asset Allocation	$947.4	$1,074.8	$800.8
Balanced	3,932.2	4,846.8	4,266.2
Flexible Portfolio	1,801.0	2,025.2	2,124.5
Income–Mixed	2,843.0	2,991.3	2,335.6
Total Hybrid Funds	**$9,523.6**	**$10,938.1**	**$9,527.1**
Corporate Bond–General	$1,219.8	$1,336.3	$1,494.0
Corporate Bond–Intermediate-term	2,560.2	3,085.6	2,299.6
Corporate Bond–Short-term	1,324.9	1,470.6	1,646.9
High-yield Bond	6,161.3	6,812.0	6,227.0
World Bond–Global General	477.6	479.0	412.2
World Bond–Global Short-term	195.5	173.5	104.3
World Bond–Other	159.6	197.3	308.9
Government Bond–General	1,299.0	1,457.4	1,292.0
Government Bond–Intermediate-term	774.7	907.2	924.0
Government Bond–Short-term	696.6	788.2	752.1
Government Bond–Mortgage-backed	2,219.8	2,500.7	2,556.0
Strategic Income	3,509.3	4,562.6	6,740.7
State Municipal Bond–General	3,149.3	3,276.5	3,107.9
State Municipal Bond–Short-term	188.4	215.9	151.0
National Municipal Bond–General	3,416.2	3,539.1	3,480.7
National Municipal Bond–Short-term	781.4	900.6	667.7
Total Bond Funds	**$28,133.6**	**$31,702.5**	**$32,165.0**

Note: Data for funds that invest in other mutual funds were excluded from the series.

Sales Less Reinvested Dividends of Equity, Hybrid, and Bond Funds by Investment Objective

(millions of dollars)

	1998	1999	2000
Total New Sales	**$997,782.0**	**$1,203,648.3**	**$1,564,382.9**
Aggressive Growth	$112,522.0	$151,402.2	$288,849.7
Growth	200,915.0	288,380.7	360,451.7
Sector	31,658.1	61,235.7	120,135.8
World Equity–Emerging Markets	7,355.1	7,222.0	11,517.5
World Equity–Global	38,438.0	46,075.0	83,748.5
World Equity–International	69,214.2	105,884.8	208,233.2
World Equity–Regional	17,739.8	22,487.8	26,812.7
Growth and Income	195,896.7	216,892.4	203,783.7
Income Equity	25,930.4	19,099.8	18,472.1
Total Equity Funds	**$699,669.3**	**$918,680.4**	**$1,322,004.9**
Asset Allocation	$6,252.1	$5,419.5	$5,887.4
Balanced	33,795.8	37,953.1	35,732.5
Flexible Portfolio	14,439.9	15,614.0	11,590.0
Income–Mixed	14,250.0	11,495.0	5,887.0
Total Hybrid Funds	**$68,737.8**	**$70,481.6**	**$59,096.9**
Corporate Bond–General	$13,157.3	$9,003.0	$9,741.0
Corporate Bond–Intermediate-term	22,376.5	21,821.7	14,557.7
Corporate Bond–Short-term	17,505.5	16,262.5	17,629.1
High-yield Bond	41,872.1	32,359.9	23,176.7
World Bond–Global General	3,979.4	3,016.0	3,312.4
World Bond–Global Short-term	1,736.3	1,403.2	1,263.3
World Bond–Other	1,870.2	1,714.1	1,708.9
Government Bond–General	9,649.2	9,079.2	7,751.1
Government Bond–Intermediate-term	7,258.1	7,988.1	5,461.5
Government Bond–Short-term	9,515.8	8,637.5	6,216.4
Government Bond–Mortgage-backed	12,183.4	12,867.4	7,298.4
Strategic Income	33,809.3	39,843.9	44,135.9
State Municipal Bond–General	22,470.9	20,042.5	14,695.3
State Municipal Bond–Short-term	2,935.2	2,888.8	2,456.9
National Municipal Bond–General	19,509.8	17,089.4	14,867.2
National Municipal Bond–Short-term	9,545.9	10,469.1	9,009.3
Total Bond Funds	**$229,374.9**	**$214,486.3**	**$183,281.1**

Note: Data for funds that invest in other mutual funds were excluded from the series.

Section Two: U.S. Industry Long-Term Funds

Equity, Hybrid, and Bond Funds Distributions to Shareholders

(millions of dollars)

Year	Dividend Distributions				Capital Gain Distributions			
	Total	Equity Funds	Hybrid Funds	Bond Funds	Total	Equity Funds	Hybrid Funds	Bond Funds
1985	$12,719.3	$3,229.0	$1,098.1	$8,392.2	$4,894.5	$3,699.3	$738.5	$456.7
1986	22,689.3	6,328.3	1,499.3	14,861.7	17,660.9	13,942.4	1,240.1	2,478.4
1987	31,707.9	7,246.4	1,933.6	22,527.9	22,925.6	18,602.8	1,604.5	2,718.3
1988	31,965.9	6,554.1	1,872.5	23,539.3	6,353.5	4,785.3	620.2	948.0
1989	34,102.4	10,235.1	2,164.9	21,702.4	14,765.8	12,664.7	539.5	1,561.6
1990	33,156.0	8,787.4	2,350.3	22,018.3	8,017.2	6,832.6	442.9	741.7
1991	35,145.0	9,007.0	2,337.1	23,800.9	13,917.2	11,961.0	861.0	1,095.2
1992	58,608.3	17,022.8	4,483.4	37,102.1	22,088.6	17,294.4	1,488.3	3,305.9
1993	73,177.6	20,230.0	6,810.2	46,137.4	35,904.6	27,704.8	3,495.8	4,704.0
1994	61,320.5	17,336.9	6,897.6	37,086.0	29,825.4	26,431.7	2,412.6	981.1
1995	67,230.7	22,567.2	9,053.5	35,610.0	54,274.5	50,203.9	3,346.8	723.8
1996	73,291.6	25,062.5	9,851.6	38,377.5	100,508.3	88,211.8	10,845.7	1,450.8
1997	79,896.2	27,971.2	11,606.7	40,318.3	183,385.8	161,365.3	19,079.9	2,940.6
1998	81,013.8	25,499.0	11,451.8	44,063.0	164,991.1	138,687.0	21,565.1	4,739.0
1999	95,443.1	32,543.8	13,100.6	49,798.7	237,624.7	219,484.5	16,841.0	1,299.2
2000	89,121.4	28,886.9	11,027.6	49,206.9	324,973.2	306,718.8	17,797.8	456.6

Note: The data contain a series break beginning in 1990. Data for funds that invest in other mutual funds were excluded from the series. Data prior to 1990 have been restated to create a consistent series back to 1985.

Annual Redemption Rate for Equity, Hybrid, and Bond Funds

(millions of dollars)

Year	Average Total Net Assets	Redemptions	Redemption Rate
1970	$47,954	$2,988	6.2%
1971	51,332	4,750	9.3
1972	57,438	6,563	11.4
1973	53,175	5,651	10.6
1974	40,290	3,381	8.4
1975	38,120	3,686	9.7
1976	44,880	6,801	15.2
1977	46,316	6,026	13.0
1978	45,014	7,232	16.1
1979	46,980	8,005	17.0
1980	53,690	8,200	15.3
1981	56,803	7,470	13.2
1982	66,024	7,572	11.5
1983	95,220	14,678	15.4
1984	125,363	20,030	16.0
1985	194,355	33,762	17.4
1986	337,551	66,970	19.8
1987	438,300	116,061	26.5
1988	462,252	92,327	20.0
1989	512,004	91,527	17.9
1990	559,719	98,071	17.5
1991	708,800	116,584	16.4
1992	973,548	165,308	17.0
1993	1,300,527	230,984	17.8
1994	1,524,548	329,232	21.6
1995	1,801,429	312,937	17.4
1996	2,341,465	397,550	17.0
1997	3,016,889	541,193	17.9
1998	3,791,423	747,680	19.7
1999	4,703,362	1,021,189	21.7
2000	5,176,574	1,334,284	25.8

Note: "Average Total Net Assets" are an average of values at the beginning of the year and at the end of the year. The redemption rate is the dollar redemption volume as a percent of average assets. The data contain a series break beginning in 1990. Data for funds that invest in other mutual funds were excluded from the series. Data prior to 1990 have been restated to create a consistent series back to 1984.

Redemptions of Equity, Hybrid, and Bond Funds
by Investment Objective
(millions of dollars)

	1998	1999	2000
Total Redemptions	**$747,680.4**	**$1,021,188.8**	**$1,334,283.9**
Aggressive Growth	$95,539.8	$125,184.3	$191,040.5
Growth	141,496.6	206,029.4	263,493.8
Sector	24,466.4	36,468.6	71,114.4
World Equity–Emerging Markets	6,915.1	6,816.1	11,259.4
World Equity–Global	31,822.0	42,334.2	63,222.8
World Equity–International	65,217.3	100,680.6	179,181.7
World Equity–Regional	15,887.4	21,406.7	28,461.7
Growth and Income	133,343.7	178,907.2	206,606.2
Income Equity	19,580.4	26,325.6	28,343.1
Total Equity Funds	**$534,268.7**	**$744,152.7**	**$1,042,723.6**
Asset Allocation	$8,507.4	$8,506.2	$7,527.1
Balanced	24,817.5	33,914.3	39,370.7
Flexible Portfolio	11,425.3	16,322.7	17,241.7
Income–Mixed	9,886.3	12,774.6	11,904.0
Total Hybrid Funds	**$54,636.5**	**$71,517.8**	**$76,043.5**
Corporate Bond–General	$7,884.6	$8,910.7	$9,671.4
Corporate Bond–Intermediate-term	13,951.8	17,192.6	15,936.8
Corporate Bond–Short-term	13,531.6	16,216.0	18,447.8
High-yield Bond	27,246.6	32,125.5	30,736.0
World Bond–Global General	4,756.1	3,947.8	3,698.2
World Bond–Global Short-term	1,861.6	1,873.2	1,852.3
World Bond–Other	1,418.2	1,952.4	2,489.2
Government Bond–General	9,326.2	10,324.8	9,857.7
Government Bond–Intermediate-term	6,181.2	6,669.8	7,178.8
Government Bond–Short-term	6,097.6	7,547.3	7,488.3
Government Bond–Mortgage-backed	9,947.3	12,305.0	13,459.6
Strategic Income	17,419.3	28,949.9	41,366.8
State Municipal Bond–General	15,392.5	22,381.3	19,947.7
State Municipal Bond–Short-term	1,811.3	2,795.0	2,129.4
National Municipal Bond–General	15,293.4	21,314.2	22,422.7
National Municipal Bond–Short-term	6,655.9	11,012.8	8,834.1
Total Bond Funds	**$158,775.2**	**$205,518.3**	**$215,516.8**

Note: Data for funds that invest in other mutual funds were excluded from the series.

Total Purchases, Total Sales, and Net Purchases of Portfolio Securities by Long-Term Mutual Funds

(millions of dollars)

Year	Total Purchases	Total Sales	Net Purchases
1970	$20,405.0	$18,588.5	$1,816.5
1971	25,360.2	24,793.8	566.4
1972	24,467.6	25,823.6	(1,356.0)
1973	19,706.6	21,903.0	(2,196.4)
1974	12,299.7	12,213.5	86.2
1975	15,396.9	15,511.4	(114.5)
1976	15,348.2	16,881.2	(1,533.0)
1977	18,168.0	19,420.7	(1,252.7)
1978	20,945.6	23,069.7	(2,124.1)
1979	22,412.1	23,702.5	(1,290.4)
1980	32,987.2	32,080.6	906.6
1981	36,161.7	33,709.2	2,452.5
1982	55,682.0	47,920.7	7,761.3
1983	93,009.5	71,466.5	21,543.0
1984	120,378.4	99,742.2	20,636.2
1985	262,472.3	188,539.3	73,933.0
1986	502,935.9	365,929.7	137,006.2
1987	538,095.8	491,428.1	46,667.7
1988	410,831.0	421,515.0	(10,684.0)
1989	471,760.2	445,459.5	26,300.7
1990	554,724.4	505,786.6	48,937.8
1991	735,682.4	608,119.7	127,562.7
1992	949,374.4	758,480.8	190,893.6
1993	1,335,567.3	1,060,396.3	275,171.0
1994	1,433,875.9	1,329,451.3	104,424.6
1995	1,550,745.0	1,400,837.4	149,907.6
1996	2,018,899.4	1,737,337.4	281,562.0
1997	2,384,639.4	2,108,980.6	275,658.8
1998	2,861,561.9	2,560,074.4	301,487.5
1999	3,437,179.7	3,224,301.2	212,878.5
2000	4,923,571.2	4,698,879.8	224,691.4

Note: The data contain a series break beginning in 1990. Data for funds that invest in other mutual funds were excluded from the series. Data prior to 1990 have been restated to create a consistent series back to 1984.

Total Purchases, Total Sales, and Net Purchases of Common Stocks by Long-Term Mutual Funds

(millions of dollars)

Year	Total Purchases	Total Sales	Net Purchases
1970	$17,127.6	$15,900.8	$1,226.8
1971	21,557.7	21,175.1	382.6
1972	20,943.5	22,552.8	(1,609.3)
1973	15,560.7	17,504.4	(1,943.7)
1974	9,085.3	9,372.1	(286.8)
1975	10,948.7	11,902.3	(953.6)
1976	10,729.1	13,278.3	(2,549.2)
1977	8,704.7	12,211.3	(3,506.6)
1978	12,832.9	14,454.7	(1,621.8)
1979	13,089.0	15,923.0	(2,834.0)
1980	19,893.8	21,799.9	(1,906.1)
1981	20,859.7	21,278.3	(418.6)
1982	27,397.2	24,939.6	2,457.6
1983	54,581.7	40,813.9	13,767.8
1984	56,584.5	50,892.1	5,692.4
1985	80,721.0	72,574.2	8,146.8
1986	134,459.8	118,033.4	16,426.4
1987	198,875.9	176,011.6	22,864.3
1988	112,742.3	128,821.7	(16,079.4)
1989	142,770.9	141,694.3	1,076.6
1990	166,401.9	146,586.3	19,815.6
1991	250,288.7	209,279.0	41,009.7
1992	327,517.7	261,857.2	65,660.6
1993	506,735.6	380,868.3	125,867.3
1994	628,715.4	512,380.6	116,334.8
1995	790,118.3	686,813.5	103,304.8
1996	1,151,439.8	927,441.0	223,998.8
1997	1,457,384.4	1,268,983.5	188,400.9
1998	1,762,565.3	1,597,310.7	165,254.6
1999	2,262,505.4	2,088,543.7	173,961.7
2000	3,561,246.1	3,331,039.5	230,206.6

Note: The data contain a series break beginning in 1990. Data for funds that invest in other mutual funds were excluded from the series. Data prior to 1990 have been restated to create a consistent series back to 1984.

Total Purchases, Total Sales, and Net Purchases of Securities Other Than Common Stocks by Long-Term Mutual Funds

(millions of dollars)

Year	Total Purchases	Total Sales	Net Purchases
1970	$3,277.4	$2,687.7	$589.7
1971	3,802.5	3,618.7	183.8
1972	3,524.1	3,270.8	253.3
1973	4,145.9	4,398.6	(252.7)
1974	3,214.4	2,841.4	373.0
1975	4,448.2	3,609.1	839.1
1976	4,619.1	3,602.9	1,016.2
1977	9,463.3	7,209.4	2,253.9
1978	8,112.7	8,615.0	(502.3)
1979	9,323.1	7,779.5	1,543.6
1980	13,093.4	10,280.7	2,812.7
1981	15,302.0	12,430.9	2,871.1
1982	28,284.8	22,981.1	5,303.7
1983	38,427.8	30,652.6	7,775.2
1984	63,793.9	48,850.1	14,943.8
1985	181,751.3	115,965.1	65,786.2
1986	368,476.1	247,896.3	120,579.8
1987	339,219.9	315,416.5	23,803.4
1988	298,088.7	292,693.3	5,395.4
1989	328,989.3	303,765.2	25,224.1
1990	388,322.5	359,200.3	29,122.2
1991	485,393.7	398,840.7	86,553.0
1992	621,856.7	496,623.6	125,233.0
1993	828,831.7	679,528.0	149,303.7
1994	805,160.5	817,070.7	(11,910.2)
1995	760,626.7	714,023.9	46,602.8
1996	867,459.6	809,896.4	57,563.2
1997	927,255.0	839,997.1	87,257.9
1998	1,098,996.6	962,763.7	136,232.9
1999	1,174,674.3	1,135,757.5	38,916.8
2000	1,362,325.1	1,367,840.3	(5,515.2)

Note: The data contain a series break beginning in 1990. Data for funds that invest in other mutual funds were excluded from the series. Data prior to 1990 have been restated to create a consistent series back to 1984.

Portfolio Purchases by Investment Objective
(millions of dollars)

	All Securities		Common Stock Only	
	1999	2000	1999	2000
Total	**$3,437,179.7**	**$4,923,571.2**	**$2,262,505.4**	**$3,561,246.1**
Aggressive Growth	$454,083.1	$869,301.0	$444,630.2	$848,477.4
Growth	784,094.6	1,193,067.5	756,742.0	1,165,713.2
Sector	132,992.1	290,744.5	130,218.3	285,960.4
World Equity–Emerging Markets	13,355.9	20,440.5	11,869.8	17,774.0
World Equity–Global	128,176.9	225,134.0	120,855.3	208,514.2
World Equity–International	130,952.8	280,807.3	123,208.4	267,088.3
World Equity–Regional	39,452.7	32,902.6	29,839.2	31,807.6
Growth and Income	484,069.6	555,355.6	453,656.6	512,275.3
Income Equity	65,643.3	70,116.5	55,833.5	59,658.4
Total Equity Funds	**$2,232,821.0**	**$3,537,869.5**	**$2,126,853.3**	**$3,397,268.8**
Asset Allocation	$38,167.4	$43,007.2	$22,407.2	$27,990.8
Balanced	146,021.4	163,040.2	69,254.4	78,923.9
Flexible Portfolio	64,243.2	74,263.8	28,719.3	41,642.3
Income–Mixed	57,397.4	39,320.4	7,824.0	7,489.3
Total Hybrid Funds	**$305,829.4**	**$319,631.6**	**$128,204.9**	**$156,046.3**
Corporate Bond–General	$41,981.9	$46,779.0	$191.5	$98.6
Corporate Bond–Intermediate-term	109,137.4	98,361.0	657.6	1,133.7
Corporate Bond–Short-term	32,277.4	29,430.7	304.4	414.6
High-yield Bond	83,377.2	62,072.9	3,214.8	3,023.0
World Bond–Global General	21,378.6	25,720.1	772.8	935.2
World Bond–Global Short-term	6,601.7	5,379.1	723.1	51.2
World Bond–Other	9,982.9	13,824.0	503.0	458.4
Government Bond–General	61,161.7	82,675.7	0.0	0.0
Government Bond–Intermediate-term	33,062.5	30,436.5	0.0	0.0
Government Bond–Short-term	42,136.2	33,847.1	0.0	0.0
Government Bond–Mortgage-backed	139,162.0	139,384.3	0.0	0.0
Strategic Income	187,963.6	394,053.2	1,080.0	1,816.3
State Municipal Bond–General	48,354.2	37,001.8	0.0	0.0
State Municipal Bond–Short-term	4,173.1	2,976.2	0.0	0.0
National Municipal Bond–General	57,026.8	48,360.7	0.0	0.0
National Municipal Bond–Short-term	20,752.1	15,767.8	0.0	0.0
Total Bond Funds	**$898,529.3**	**$1,066,070.1**	**$7,447.2**	**$7,931.0**

Note: Data for funds that invest in other mutual funds were excluded from the series.

Portfolio Sales by Investment Objective

(millions of dollars)

	All Securities		Common Stock Only	
	1999	2000	1999	2000
Total	**$3,224,301.2**	**$4,698,879.8**	**$2,088,543.7**	**$3,331,039.5**
Aggressive Growth	$418,860.5	$766,926.9	$409,657.9	$747,586.1
Growth	698,143.8	1,088,946.3	672,908.2	1,060,024.8
Sector	108,348.2	237,706.8	106,263.4	233,586.2
World Equity–Emerging Markets	12,011.3	20,748.3	10,810.2	18,061.5
World Equity–Global	122,808.9	202,325.7	114,978.3	188,454.5
World Equity–International	128,837.2	255,458.6	120,470.4	241,815.7
World Equity–Regional	38,295.2	36,775.9	27,885.7	35,688.3
Growth and Income	447,177.8	587,634.4	414,151.4	548,976.9
Income Equity	75,055.7	90,096.3	64,378.2	78,827.6
Total Equity Funds	**$2,049,538.6**	**$3,286,619.2**	**$1,941,503.7**	**$3,153,021.6**
Asset Allocation	$42,624.9	$44,795.0	$24,237.7	$29,943.1
Balanced	142,725.8	167,915.2	71,936.8	84,390.2
Flexible Portfolio	63,433.9	80,565.4	34,352.7	42,881.9
Income–Mixed	55,902.1	47,537.5	8,197.1	11,189.2
Total Hybrid Funds	**$304,686.7**	**$340,813.1**	**$138,724.3**	**$168,404.4**
Corporate Bond–General	$41,287.8	$45,001.0	$190.1	$106.5
Corporate Bond–Intermediate-term	102,477.4	97,425.1	746.1	1,186.6
Corporate Bond–Short-term	28,847.6	28,021.3	276.7	781.1
High-yield Bond	79,052.6	72,365.7	3,584.4	3,385.0
World Bond–Global General	22,196.8	25,360.0	967.0	938.7
World Bond–Global Short-term	6,846.8	5,741.3	786.3	45.2
World Bond–Other	10,406.8	14,463.9	554.4	548.5
Government Bond–General	61,347.5	83,666.8	0.0	0.0
Government Bond–Intermediate-term	31,580.7	31,286.3	0.0	0.0
Government Bond–Short-term	40,796.2	36,872.5	0.0	0.0
Government Bond–Mortgage-backed	134,777.1	140,585.8	0.0	0.0
Strategic Income	177,209.5	377,091.5	1,210.7	2,621.9
State Municipal Bond–General	50,258.4	40,723.5	0.0	0.0
State Municipal Bond–Short-term	3,705.7	3,375.6	0.0	0.0
National Municipal Bond–General	60,310.5	53,620.1	0.0	0.0
National Municipal Bond–Short-term	18,974.5	15,847.1	0.0	0.0
Total Bond Funds	**$870,075.9**	**$1,071,447.5**	**$8,315.7**	**$9,613.5**

Note: Data for funds that invest in other mutual funds were excluded from the series.

Section Three: U.S. Industry Short-Term Funds

Total Short-Term Funds
(millions of dollars)

Year	Total Sales	Total Redemptions	Net Sales	Net New Cash Flow*	Dividend Distributions	Number of Funds	Total Accounts Outstanding	Total Net Assets
1980	$237,427.7	$207,877.7	$29,550.0	$24,022.7	$7,765.7	106	4,762,103	$76,361.3
1981	462,422.6	354,972.1	107,450.5	91,143.7	18,573.3	179	10,323,466	186,158.2
1982	611,202.9	580,778.4	30,424.5	9,184.1	21,980.0	318	13,258,143	219,837.5
1983	507,447.0	551,151.3	(43,704.3)	(55,664.9)	13,782.3	373	12,539,688	179,386.5
1984	634,226.7	586,992.4	47,234.3	35,062.4	16,434.9	421	13,844,697	233,553.8
1985	839,498.8	831,121.2	8,377.6	(5,381.8)	15,707.7	457	14,934,631	243,802.4
1986	989,816.0	948,641.3	41,174.7	33,861.8	14,832.1	485	16,313,148	292,151.6
1987	1,060,949.2	1,062,519.7	(1,570.5)	10,191.2	15,654.0	541	17,674,790	316,096.1
1988	1,081,702.0	1,074,373.5	7,328.5	74.7	21,618.1	605	18,569,817	337,956.5
1989	1,319,492.6	1,235,643.0	83,849.6	64,053.4	28,618.8	664	21,314,228	428,093.2
1990	1,415,701.4	1,372,725.2	42,976.2	23,219.6	30,257.9	741	22,968,817	498,341.3
1991	1,800,758.0	1,763,106.3	37,651.7	5,499.0	28,604.3	820	23,556,000	542,441.6
1992	2,386,288.1	2,382,986.3	3,301.7	(16,299.6)	20,279.7	864	23,647,186	546,194.5
1993	2,677,539.5	2,673,464.4	4,075.1	(14,110.2)	18,991.3	920	23,585,329	565,319.1
1994	2,603,333.8	2,598,992.9	4,341.0	8,767.0	23,736.6	963	25,378,671	611,004.5
1995	3,125,209.0	3,001,928.0	123,281.0	89,411.1	37,037.7	997	30,136,777	753,017.7
1996	3,990,530.5	3,868,771.7	121,758.9	89,421.8	42,554.8	988	32,199,937	901,807.0
1997	4,930,584.6	4,782,897.7	147,686.9	102,069.4	48,842.6	1,013	35,624,081	1,058,885.7
1998	6,172,574.8	5,901,591.3	270,983.5	235,335.2	57,375.5	1,026	38,847,345	1,351,678.3
1999	7,769,960.3	7,540,911.8	229,048.5	193,630.4	69,004.0	1,045	43,615,576	1,613,145.5
2000	9,479,064.5	9,256,074.8	222,989.7	159,647.8	98,219.3	1,041	48,138,665	1,845,295.1

*Net new cash flow is the dollar value of new sales minus redemptions, combined with net exchanges.

An Overview: Taxable Money Market Funds

(millions of dollars)

Year	Total Sales	Total Redemptions	Net Sales	Net New Cash Flow*	Dividend Distributions	Number of Funds	Total Accounts Outstanding	Average Maturity (days)	Total Net Assets
1980	$232,172.8	$204,068.5	$28,104.3	$22,527.6	$7,665.7	96	4,745,572	24	$74,447.7
1981	451,889.5	346,701.5	105,188.0	88,939.7	18,473.3	159	10,282,095	34	181,910.4
1982	581,758.9	559,581.1	22,177.8	1,704.2	21,680.0	281	13,101,347	37	206,607.5
1983	462,978.7	508,729.9	(45,751.2)	(57,437.5)	13,182.3	307	12,276,639	37	162,549.5
1984	571,959.3	531,050.9	40,908.4	29,163.5	15,434.9	326	13,556,180	43	209,731.9
1985	730,073.8	732,343.0	(2,269.2)	(15,884.1)	14,107.7	346	14,435,386	42	207,535.3
1986	792,349.1	776,303.2	16,045.9	9,028.8	12,432.1	359	15,653,595	45	228,345.8
1987	869,099.1	865,668.4	3,430.7	13,054.6	12,832.9	388	16,832,666	34	254,676.4
1988	903,425.9	899,397.3	4,028.6	(1,512.4)	17,976.0	431	17,630,528	31	272,293.3
1989	1,134,647.8	1,055,142.4	79,505.4	62,537.5	24,682.9	463	20,173,265	40	358,719.2
1990	1,218,935.9	1,183,085.9	35,850.1	17,433.2	26,447.6	506	21,577,559	47	414,733.3
1991	1,569,852.0	1,536,509.6	33,342.4	4,420.8	25,120.9	553	21,863,352	56	452,559.2
1992	2,099,796.8	2,101,420.8	(1,624.0)	(20,468.2)	17,196.9	585	21,770,693	58	451,353.4
1993	2,335,653.0	2,336,939.6	(1,286.7)	(19,122.8)	15,689.5	628	21,586,862	59	461,903.9
1994	2,234,069.0	2,229,036.6	5,032.4	7,932.4	20,500.2	646	23,339,838	38	500,635.5
1995	2,729,117.5	2,617,221.3	111,896.2	82,127.1	32,822.2	674	27,859,258	57	629,985.8
1996	3,523,786.6	3,415,494.5	108,292.1	79,186.0	38,363.9	666	29,907,471	54	761,989.0
1997	4,394,583.3	4,265,341.8	129,241.5	86,649.7	44,109.6	682	32,960,628	55	898,083.1
1998	5,533,565.3	5,289,265.8	244,299.4	212,408.3	52,072.4	685	36,442,150	56	1,163,166.7
1999	7,083,029.5	6,865,682.3	217,347.2	182,795.8	63,107.4	702	41,177,138	49	1,408,731.0
2000	8,690,835.2	8,499,013.2	191,822.0	133,121.6	89,955.8	704	45,479,747	51	1,607,240.6

*Net new cash flow is the dollar value of new sales minus redemptions, combined with net exchanges.

Section Three: U.S. Industry Short-Term Funds

An Overview: Tax-Exempt Money Market Funds

(millions of dollars)

Year		Total Sales	Total Redemptions	Net Sales	Net New Cash Flow*	Dividend Distributions	Number of Funds	Total Accounts Outstanding	Total Net Assets
1987	National	$179,215.0	$185,031.1	($5,816.1)	($4,926.4)	$2,600.8	111	731,265	$54,555.8
	State	12,635.1	11,820.2	814.9	2,063.0	220.3	42	110,859	6,863.9
1988	National	158,085.8	158,120.8	(35.0)	(2,214.3)	2,990.1	120	754,068	54,541.7
	State	20,190.4	16,855.5	3,334.9	3,801.4	652.0	54	185,221	11,118.5
1989	National	152,713.4	151,851.4	862.0	(2,053.4)	3,011.1	129	875,626	52,824.7
	State	32,131.3	28,649.2	3,482.1	3,569.4	924.8	72	265,337	16,549.4
1990	National	155,956.9	153,363.8	2,593.1	1,162.5	2,688.9	133	984,301	59,200.5
	State	40,808.5	36,275.6	4,532.9	4,623.9	1,121.4	102	406,957	24,407.6
1991	National	181,137.9	178,927.1	2,210.8	474.1	2,463.2	141	1,139,741	62,338.0
	State	49,768.1	47,669.6	2,098.5	604.1	1,020.2	126	552,907	27,544.5
1992	National	223,414.2	220,832.0	2,582.3	2,659.5	2,171.5	139	1,120,735	64,863.3
	State	63,077.0	60,733.5	2,343.5	1,509.1	911.3	140	755,758	29,977.9
1993	National	264,844.1	261,686.2	3,157.9	2,753.6	2,024.1	145	1,237,326	70,451.2
	State	77,042.5	74,838.6	2,203.9	2,259.0	1,277.7	147	761,141	32,964.6
1994	National	281,800.3	283,647.0	(1,846.7)	(932.6)	1,810.3	154	1,267,090	73,120.1
	State	87,464.6	86,309.3	1,155.3	1,767.1	1,426.1	163	771,743	37,248.9
1995	National	291,273.2	286,223.2	5,050.0	2,449.7	2,832.0	154	1,377,008	79,227.4
	State	104,818.3	98,483.5	6,334.8	4,834.3	1,383.5	169	900,511	43,804.5
1996	National	340,669.6	334,148.6	6,521.0	4,359.5	2,795.9	155	1,346,220	88,845.7
	State	126,074.3	119,128.6	6,945.8	5,876.3	1,395.0	167	946,246	50,972.3
1997	National	383,863.2	373,233.5	10,629.7	8,939.7	3,059.7	156	1,557,399	100,911.3
	State	152,138.1	144,322.4	7,815.7	6,480.0	1,673.3	175	1,106,054	59,891.3
1998	National	452,774.4	437,679.8	15,094.5	13,100.6	3,446.3	155	1,284,287	117,374.0
	State	186,235.2	174,645.6	11,589.5	9,826.3	1,856.8	186	1,120,908	71,137.6
1999	National	474,581.0	470,076.8	4,504.2	4,545.9	3,709.0	158	1,310,161	125,397.3
	State	212,349.7	205,152.8	7,197.0	6,288.7	2,187.6	185	1,128,277	79,017.2
2000	National	533,978.0	513,080.9	20,897.1	17,866.9	5,256.0	151	1,411,570	145,280.9
	State	254,251.3	243,980.7	10,270.6	8,659.3	3,007.5	186	1,247,348	92,773.6

*Net new cash flow is the dollar value of new sales minus redemptions, combined with net exchanges.

Taxable Money Market Fund Monthly Total Net Assets
by Type of Fund
(thousands of dollars)

	Individual	Institutional	Total
1998			
January	$541,736,108	$386,851,460	$928,587,568
February	558,096,614	395,267,596	953,364,210
March	571,446,356	395,975,981	967,422,337
April	566,224,539	404,786,101	971,010,640
May	580,637,625	414,139,292	994,776,917
June	582,274,631	412,897,380	995,172,011
July	594,941,847	420,653,673	1,015,595,520
August	626,401,648	441,589,555	1,067,991,203
September	632,259,350	453,794,810	1,086,054,160
October	654,352,422	477,132,799	1,131,485,221
November	663,366,187	501,843,017	1,165,209,204
December	668,870,385	494,296,330	1,163,166,715
1999			
January	$687,392,158	$531,173,129	$1,218,565,287
February	707,230,347	535,929,425	1,243,159,772
March	715,778,080	522,772,065	1,238,550,145
April	708,031,292	521,485,758	1,229,517,050
May	706,870,696	530,347,234	1,237,217,930
June	705,927,639	523,446,737	1,229,374,376
July	716,513,479	534,149,652	1,250,663,131
August	731,851,214	552,689,185	1,284,540,399
September	737,625,947	545,939,984	1,283,565,931
October	742,125,744	581,169,056	1,323,294,800
November	765,459,578	608,202,442	1,373,662,020
December	774,645,319	634,085,681	1,408,731,000
2000			
January	$800,320,727	$644,747,466	$1,445,068,193
February	812,432,623	653,132,008	1,465,564,631
March	835,438,929	640,261,873	1,475,700,802
April	812,083,214	628,283,718	1,440,366,932
May	811,672,056	647,693,501	1,459,365,557
June	797,559,525	646,084,068	1,443,643,593
July	806,707,155	670,240,141	1,476,947,296
August	813,483,214	692,952,736	1,506,435,950
September	814,849,812	692,492,103	1,507,341,915
October	818,407,433	715,751,976	1,534,159,409
November	838,536,028	749,677,590	1,588,213,618
December	846,489,518	760,751,044	1,607,240,562

Taxable Money Market Fund
Shareholder Accounts by Type of Fund

	Individual	Institutional	Total
1998			
January	29,835,970	2,942,434	32,778,404
February	30,228,820	2,942,808	33,171,628
March	30,389,255	3,010,853	33,400,108
April	30,715,289	3,062,307	33,777,596
May	31,353,479	3,044,806	34,398,285
June	32,765,377	3,071,555	35,836,932
July	31,830,339	3,206,041	35,036,380
August	32,722,981	3,268,267	35,991,248
September	32,638,562	3,316,897	35,955,459
October	33,014,433	3,248,164	36,262,597
November	33,385,847	3,229,880	36,615,727
December	33,144,698	3,297,452	36,442,150
1999			
January	33,852,847	3,339,405	37,192,252
February	34,379,272	3,340,902	37,720,174
March	34,451,497	3,353,784	37,805,281
April	34,826,780	3,426,882	38,253,662
May	35,402,788	3,434,689	38,837,477
June	35,601,788	3,531,522	39,133,310
July	36,000,523	3,957,345	39,957,868
August	36,324,068	4,070,097	40,394,165
September	36,207,987	4,145,864	40,353,851
October	36,546,644	4,282,828	40,829,472
November	37,118,077	4,271,042	41,389,119
December	36,979,698	4,197,440	41,177,138
2000			
January	37,201,437	3,894,684	41,096,121
February	37,555,281	3,826,930	41,382,211
March	38,941,031	3,891,413	42,832,444
April	39,419,053	3,569,971	42,989,024
May	39,579,937	4,039,662	43,619,599
June	38,671,054	3,899,253	42,570,307
July	38,699,735	3,835,729	42,535,464
August	38,807,825	3,867,723	42,675,548
September	40,689,801	4,302,046	44,991,847
October	40,539,919	4,351,546	44,891,465
November	41,121,395	4,448,092	45,569,487
December	41,046,136	4,433,611	45,479,747

Taxable Money Market Fund Asset Composition

(millions of dollars)

	1995	1996	1997	1998	1999	2000
Total Net Assets	**$629,985.8**	**$761,989.0**	**$898,083.1**	**$1,163,166.7**	**$1,408,731.0**	**$1,607,240.6**
U.S. Treasury Bills	42,280.8	42,195.0	40,955.2	48,115.7	60,054.7	54,515.4
Other Treasury Securities	29,347.6	49,644.1	47,934.1	62,005.4	46,311.1	37,843.0
U.S. Securities	92,752.0	104,189.2	97,804.1	176,043.0	195,734.0	189,095.2
Repurchase Agreements	89,316.2	105,710.6	128,901.5	141,710.8	143,975.3	186,890.2
Certificates of Deposits	39,898.6	69,316.8	95,565.7	111,908.4	138,984.6	122,573.8
Eurodollar CDs	20,066.2	23,569.3	23,951.8	30,713.8	42,095.9	93,026.8
Commercial Paper	237,121.9	276,801.4	339,501.0	420,975.0	535,288.5	619,718.7
Bank Notes	16,727.7	12,398.3	21,017.4	33,668.5	33,828.2	46,120.5
Bankers Acceptances	3,059.6	2,619.9	3,472.6	2,860.5	2,884.3	1,782.5
Corporate Notes	0.0	0.0	0.0	50,255.0	94,010.8	119,175.6
Cash Reserves	(3,596.0)	(1,159.2)	1,479.5	(1,046.9)	(3,392.7)	2,276.1
Other Assets	63,011.2	76,703.6	97,500.2	85,957.5	118,956.3	134,222.8
Average Maturity (days)	57	54	55	56	49	51
Number of Funds	674	666	682	685	702	704

Note: Prior to 1998, corporate notes are included in the "Other Assets" category.

Sales Due to Exchanges by Investment Objective
(millions of dollars)

	1998	1999	2000
Total	**$742,855.5**	**$949,940.3**	**$1,149,770.4**
Aggressive Growth	$84,596.3	$122,117.6	$193,321.4
Growth	91,807.7	128,962.1	162,319.0
Sector	41,172.7	53,726.9	84,483.7
World Equity–Emerging Markets	1,510.1	3,213.9	5,254.7
World Equity–Global	24,477.1	38,729.1	52,298.9
World Equity–International	31,455.4	53,143.1	75,843.6
World Equity–Regional	19,937.9	16,355.9	15,681.6
Growth and Income	60,457.5	68,447.5	57,939.0
Income Equity	10,370.8	7,636.4	6,914.1
Total Equity Funds	**$365,785.5**	**$492,332.5**	**$654,056.0**
Asset Allocation	$2,554.2	$2,467.2	$2,912.9
Balanced	7,558.1	8,078.0	6,630.1
Flexible Portfolio	2,635.3	2,274.4	2,340.7
Income–Mixed	2,739.5	1,515.5	1,577.1
Total Hybrid Funds	**$15,487.1**	**$14,335.1**	**$13,460.8**
Corporate Bond–General	$3,067.0	$2,476.0	$2,285.1
Corporate Bond–Intermediate-term	6,188.7	5,330.5	3,263.2
Corporate Bond–Short-term	3,849.9	5,687.0	3,633.2
High-yield Bond	13,919.6	13,000.2	10,270.3
World Bond–Global General	1,799.2	972.7	959.6
World Bond–Global Short-term	649.6	104.6	93.2
World Bond–Other	491.6	316.0	342.4
Government Bond–General	6,078.5	5,785.6	3,615.1
Government Bond–Intermediate-term	4,670.3	4,262.3	2,854.8
Government Bond–Short-term	3,882.3	5,243.5	3,016.3
Government Bond–Mortgage-backed	6,160.7	7,850.2	7,232.9
Strategic Income	8,162.0	6,575.4	8,122.8
State Municipal Bond–General	6,971.7	6,383.4	5,121.1
State Municipal Bond–Short-term	513.3	601.0	187.7
National Municipal Bond–General	14,828.1	14,004.5	8,992.3
National Municipal Bond–Short-term	2,030.1	3,051.1	1,873.0
Total Bond Funds	**$83,262.6**	**$81,644.0**	**$61,863.0**
Taxable Money Market–Government	$29,338.1	$50,027.5	$45,339.5
Taxable Money Market–Non-government	232,955.9	289,513.4	356,444.1
National Tax-exempt Money Market	11,541.2	16,250.5	12,403.7
State Tax-exempt Money Market	4,485.1	5,837.3	6,203.3
Total Money Market Funds	**$278,320.3**	**$361,628.7**	**$420,390.6**

Note: Data for funds that invest in other mutual funds were excluded from the series.

Redemptions Due to Exchanges by Investment Objective
(millions of dollars)

	1998	1999	2000
Total	**$743,366.6**	**$947,387.8**	**$1,141,235.3**
Aggressive Growth	$89,914.6	$113,995.3	$161,803.5
Growth	86,971.0	114,311.8	140,197.7
Sector	41,535.0	49,545.6	71,194.5
World Equity–Emerging Markets	1,851.2	2,855.9	5,404.3
World Equity–Global	26,795.6	39,378.7	50,108.0
World Equity–International	34,621.3	52,360.5	73,372.0
World Equity–Regional	19,490.7	16,054.5	18,471.7
Growth and Income	61,117.0	75,772.2	87,098.1
Income Equity	11,857.3	14,920.0	16,099.4
Total Equity Funds	**$374,153.7**	**$479,194.5**	**$623,749.2**
Asset Allocation	$4,483.2	$4,617.0	$4,275.8
Balanced	8,458.5	12,257.1	15,230.5
Flexible Portfolio	3,031.3	3,952.9	3,870.9
Income–Mixed	3,461.3	4,823.8	4,921.1
Total Hybrid Funds	**$19,434.3**	**$25,650.8**	**$28,298.3**
Corporate Bond–General	$2,594.2	$3,073.6	$2,940.9
Corporate Bond–Intermediate-term	4,415.2	5,968.4	3,993.5
Corporate Bond–Short-term	3,646.3	4,999.8	4,060.2
High-yield Bond	14,943.5	15,780.5	14,943.8
World Bond–Global General	2,328.6	1,463.9	1,443.7
World Bond–Global Short-term	695.8	193.8	113.5
World Bond–Other	621.8	466.2	432.9
Government Bond–General	5,249.2	7,160.0	4,791.9
Government Bond–Intermediate-term	3,394.9	4,734.4	3,431.3
Government Bond–Short-term	4,459.4	6,726.5	5,202.2
Government Bond–Mortgage-backed	5,843.8	8,221.1	8,393.5
Strategic Income	6,607.3	8,174.3	10,454.2
State Municipal Bond–General	7,285.1	8,647.1	5,609.2
State Municipal Bond–Short-term	403.1	675.3	287.4
National Municipal Bond–General	14,867.0	16,789.5	10,000.8
National Municipal Bond–Short-term	1,897.4	3,071.6	2,127.5
Total Bond Funds	**$79,252.6**	**$96,146.0**	**$78,226.5**
Taxable Money Market–Government	$26,875.9	$46,285.4	$46,013.7
Taxable Money Market–Non-government	227,799.1	281,290.9	347,690.6
National Tax-exempt Money Market	11,037.6	13,640.3	11,682.5
State Tax-exempt Money Market	4,813.4	5,179.9	5,574.5
Total Money Market Funds	**$270,526.0**	**$346,396.5**	**$410,961.3**

Note: Data for funds that invest in other mutual funds were excluded from the series.

Net Sales Due to Exchanges by Investment Objective
(millions of dollars)

	1998	1999	2000
Total	**($511.1)**	**$2,552.5**	**$8,535.1**
Aggressive Growth	($5,318.3)	$8,122.3	$31,517.9
Growth	4,836.7	14,650.3	22,121.3
Sector	(362.3)	4,181.3	13,289.2
World Equity–Emerging Markets	(341.1)	358.0	(149.6)
World Equity–Global	(2,318.5)	(649.6)	2,190.9
World Equity–International	(3,165.9)	782.6	2,471.6
World Equity–Regional	447.2	301.4	(2,790.1)
Growth and Income	(659.5)	(7,324.7)	(29,159.1)
Income Equity	(1,486.5)	(7,283.6)	(9,185.3)
Total Equity Funds	**($8,368.2)**	**$13,138.0**	**$30,306.8**
Asset Allocation	($1,929.0)	($2,149.8)	($1,362.9)
Balanced	(900.4)	(4,179.1)	(8,600.4)
Flexible Portfolio	(396.0)	(1,678.5)	(1,530.2)
Income–Mixed	(721.8)	(3,308.4)	(3,344.0)
Total Hybrid Funds	**($3,947.2)**	**($11,315.8)**	**($14,837.5)**
Corporate Bond–General	$472.8	($597.6)	($655.8)
Corporate Bond–Intermediate-term	1,773.5	(637.9)	(730.3)
Corporate Bond–Short-term	203.6	687.2	(427.0)
High-yield Bond	(1,023.9)	(2,780.3)	(4,673.5)
World Bond–Global General	(529.4)	(491.2)	(484.1)
World Bond–Global Short-term	(46.2)	(89.2)	(20.3)
World Bond–Other	(130.2)	(150.2)	(90.5)
Government Bond–General	829.3	(1,374.4)	(1,176.8)
Government Bond–Intermediate-term	1,275.4	(472.1)	(576.5)
Government Bond–Short-term	(577.1)	(1,483.0)	(2,185.9)
Government Bond–Mortgage-backed	316.9	(370.9)	(1,160.6)
Strategic Income	1,554.7	(1,598.9)	(2,331.4)
State Municipal Bond–General	(313.4)	(2,263.6)	(488.1)
State Municipal Bond–Short-term	110.2	(74.3)	(99.7)
National Municipal Bond–General	(38.9)	(2,785.0)	(1,008.5)
National Municipal Bond–Short-term	132.7	(20.5)	(254.5)
Total Bond Funds	**$4,010.0**	**($14,501.9)**	**($16,363.5)**
Taxable Money Market–Government	$2,462.2	$3,742.1	($674.2)
Taxable Money Market–Non-government	5,156.8	8,222.5	8,753.5
National Tax-exempt Money Market	503.6	2,610.2	721.2
State Tax-exempt Money Market	(328.3)	657.4	628.8
Total Money Market Funds	**$7,794.3**	**$15,232.2**	**$9,429.3**

Note: Data for funds that invest in other mutual funds were excluded from the series.

Section Five: Institutional Investors in the U.S. Industry

Assets of Major Institutions and Financial Intermediaries
(millions of dollars)

	1994	1995	1996	1997	1998	1999	2000
Depository Institutions	**$5,461,950.0**	**$5,817,216.0**	**$6,072,189.0**	**$6,557,007.0**	**$7,122,098.0**	**$7,555,261.0**	**$8,116,326.0**
Commercial Banks[a]	4,159,707.0[R]	4,493,798.0[R]	4,710,397.0[R]	5,174,550.0	5,642,181.0[R]	5,989,322.0[R]	6,455,626.0
Credit Unions[b]	293,597.0[R]	310,661.0[R]	330,114.0[R]	353,831.0[R]	391,483.0[R]	414,527.0[R]	441,620.0
Savings Institutions[c]	1,008,646.0[R]	1,012,757.0[R]	1,031,678.0[R]	1,028,626.0[R]	1,088,434.0[R]	1,151,412.0[R]	1,219,080.0
Life Insurance	**1,862,888.0[R]**	**2,063,613.0[R]**	**2,246,289.0[R]**	**2,514,802.0[R]**	**2,769,522.0[R]**	**3,067,922.0[R]**	**3,133,910.0**
Investment Institutions	**4,311,878.3**	**5,391,975.6**	**6,353,023.0**	**7,982,754.7**	**9,677,672.8**	**11,391,835.5[R]**	**7,100,060.4**
Bank-administered Trusts[d]	2,043,197.2[R]	2,444,822.9	2,684,453.4	3,364,446.6	3,999,320.7	4,380,797.8[R]	N/A
Closed-end Investment Companies	113,285.1	135,668.7	142,299.6	150,107.5	153,142.8[R]	164,698.5[R]	134,811.3[e]
Mutual Funds[f]	2,155,396.0	2,811,484.0	3,526,270.0	4,468,200.6	5,525,209.3	6,846,339.2	6,965,249.1

[a]Includes U.S.-chartered commercial banks, foreign banking offices in the U.S., bank holding companies, and banks in affiliated areas.

[b]Includes only federal or federally insured state credit unions serving natural persons.

[c]Includes mutual savings banks, federal savings banks, and savings & loan associations.

[d]Reflects only discretionary trusts and agencies.

[e]Preliminary data.

[f]Includes short-term funds; excludes funds of funds.

[R]Revised

N/A=Not available

Source: Federal Reserve Board, Federal Financial Institutions Examination Council, and Investment Company Institute

Assets of Fiduciary, Business, and Other Institutional Investors*

(millions of dollars)

Equity, Hybrid, and Bond Funds

	1998	1999	2000P
Fiduciaries (Banks and Individuals Serving as Trustees, Guardians, and Administrators)	**$390,780.8**	**$460,590.5**	**$387,015.9**
Business Organizations	**1,424,857.3**	**1,874,652.3**	**1,799,737.5**
Business Corporations	95,484.3	128,892.8	129,150.0
Retirement Plans	861,446.9	1,126,304.2	1,071,472.9
Insurance Companies and Other Financial Institutions	467,926.1	619,455.3	599,114.7
Nonprofit Organizations	**41,069.0**	**50,752.4**	**53,589.7**
Other Institutional Investors Not Classified**	**17,658.6**	**28,404.1**	**30,869.5**
Total	**$1,874,365.8**	**$2,414,399.3**	**$2,271,212.6**

Note: Reporters of institutional data represented 82.4% of total assets in 1998, 82.2 % in 1999, and 84.4% in 2000.

Taxable Money Market Funds

	1998	1999	2000P
Fiduciaries (Banks and Individuals Serving as Trustees, Guardians, and Administrators)	**$185,823.0**	**$220,917.3**	**$255,343.8**
Business Organizations	**332,943.4**	**425,003.2**	**498,519.7**
Business Corporations	136,643.0	169,022.6	218,722.6
Retirement Plans	70,328.2	83,229.2	87,470.1
Insurance Companies and Other Financial Institutions	125,972.1	172,751.4	192,327.0
Nonprofit Organizations	**15,913.2**	**15,947.9**	**18,525.2**
Other Institutional Investors Not Classified**	**15,305.3**	**28,156.0**	**33,718.8**
Total	**$549,985.0**	**$690,024.4**	**$806,107.5**

Note: Reporters of institutional data represented 56.5% of total assets in 1998, 59.6% in 1999, and 64.1% in 2000.

Tax-exempt Money Market Funds

	1998	1999	2000P
Fiduciaries (Banks and Individuals Serving as Trustees, Guardians, and Administrators)	**$34,339.8**	**$34,699.8**	**$43,246.6**
Business Organizations	**20,969.5**	**21,329.9**	**23,452.2**
Business Corporations	10,175.9	10,848.0	11,556.3
Retirement Plans	417.8	429.6	439.4
Insurance Companies and Other Financial Institutions	10,375.8	10,052.4	11,456.5
Nonprofit Organizations	**1,479.6**	**547.7**	**582.4**
Other Institutional Investors Not Classified**	**748.4**	**1,254.4**	**2,587.5**
Total	**$57,537.3**	**$57,831.8**	**$69,868.7**

Note: Tax-exempt money market fund reporters represented 58.6% of total net assets in 1998, 64.3% in 1999, and 66.2% in 2000.

*Data for funds that invest in other mutual funds were excluded from the series.

PPreliminary data.

**Includes institutional assets for which no determination can be made.

Note: Components may not sum to the total due to rounding.

Assets of Fiduciary, Business, and Other Institutional Investors in Taxable Money Market Funds by Type of Fund

(millions of dollars)

	Individual			Institutional		
	1998	1999	2000ᴾ	1998	1999	2000ᴾ
Fiduciaries (Banks and Individuals Serving as Trustees, Guardians, and Administrators)	$83,270.1	$101,673.8	$112,548.8	$102,552.9	$119,243.5	$142,795.0
Business Organizations	102,475.3	111,356.4	128,395.8	230,468.1	313,646.9	370,124.0
Business Corporations	47,642.3	47,111.2	63,534.6	89,000.7	121,911.5	155,188.1
Retirement Plans	37,817.9	42,339.6	43,151.2	32,510.4	40,889.6	44,318.9
Insurance Companies and Other Financial Institutions	17,015.1	21,905.6	21,710.0	108,957.0	150,845.8	170,617.1
Nonprofit Organizations	5,908.1	6,953.0	8,092.3	10,005.1	8,994.8	10,433.0
Other Institutional Investors Not Classified*	6,498.1	8,891.1	10,822.6	8,807.2	19,264.9	22,896.3
Total	$198,151.6	$228,874.3	$259,859.5	$351,833.3	$461,150.1	$546,248.2

ᴾPreliminary data.

*Includes institutional accounts for which no determination of classification can be made.

Components may not sum to the total due to rounding

Worldwide Assets of Open-End Investment Companies
(millions of U.S. dollars)

NON-USA COUNTRIES	1995	1996	1997	1998	1999	2000[a]
Argentina	$631	$1,869	$5,247	$6,930	$6,990	$7,664
Australia	36,505	47,761	42,909	44,124[b]	N/A	328,062
Austria[c]	33,452	39,543	44,930	63,772	75,730	76,422
Belgium	25,553	29,247	33,658	56,339	65,461	65,683
Brazil	63,637	103,786	108,606	118,687	117,758	151,091
Canada[c]	107,812	154,529	197,985	213,451	269,825	287,783
Chile	2,843	2,934	4,549	2,910	4,091	4,431[d]
Czech Republic	N/A	N/A	361	556	1,473	1,754
Denmark	6,455	9,338	13,037	19,450	27,545	30,739
Finland	1,211	2,510	3,534	5,695	10,318	12,961
France	519,376	534,145	495,774	626,154	656,132	686,569
Germany Public	134,543	137,860	146,888	195,701	237,312	240,815
Special	213,047	241,642[e]	N/A	N/A	N/A	N/A
Greece	10,303	15,788	25,759	32,194	36,397	29,517
Hong Kong	33,695	41,017	58,456	98,767	182,265	222,963
Hungary	N/A	N/A	713	1,476	1,725	2,004
India	10,107	9,717[f]	9,353	8,685	13,065	12,963
Ireland[g]	8,461	7,735	22,729	22,520[h]	95,135	131,160
Italy	79,878	129,992	209,410	439,701	478,530	418,874
Japan	469,980	420,103	311,335	376,533	502,752	491,852
Korea	92,405	N/A	N/A	N/A	167,177	124,865
Luxembourg	285,448	338,236	390,623	N/A	659,284	727,376
Mexico	9,025[i]	N/A	N/A	N/A	19,468	19,011
Netherlands[c]	62,128	67,147	70,373	87,996	102,492	N/A
New Zealand[c]	6,868	7,686	7,519	7,250	8,502	7,258
Norway	6,834	9,930	13,058	11,148	15,107	16,195
Philippines	N/A	N/A	N/A	N/A	117	123
Poland	282	475	541	517	762	1,279
Portugal	14,233	17,079	15,472	23,299	20,574	17,005
Russia	N/A	6	41	29	177	245
South Africa	9,226	9,354	12,688	12,160	18,235	17,580
Spain	99,923	144,134	177,192	238,917	207,603	171,751
Sweden	27,388	34,981	45,452	54,923	83,250	78,989
Switzerland	44,638	48,166	53,444	69,151	82,512	82,712
Taiwan	4,388	8,351[f]	12,365	20,310	31,153	38,896
United Kingdom[j]	154,452	201,304	235,683	283,711	370,962	376,831
TOTAL NON-USA	**2,574,727**	**2,816,365**	**2,769,684**	**3,143,056**	**4,569,879**	**4,883,423**
USA[j] (long-term)	2,058,466	2,624,463	3,409,315	4,173,531	5,233,194	5,541,430
(short-term)	753,018	901,807	1,058,886	1,351,678	1,613,145	1,727,690
TOTAL USA	**2,811,484**	**3,526,270**	**4,468,201**	**5,525,209**	**6,846,339**	**7,269,120**
TOTAL WORLD	**$5,386,211**	**$6,342,635**	**$7,237,885**	**$8,668,265**	**$11,416,218**	**$12,152,543**

[a]As of September 30, 2000, unless otherwise noted.
[b]As of September 30, 1998.
[c]Includes real estate funds.
[d]As of June 30, 2000.
[e]As of September 30, 1996.
[f]As of June 30, 1996.
[g]Approximately 95 percent relates to life assurance-linked funds; the other 5 percent are unit investment trusts. International Financial Service Center funds are not included.
[h]As of March 31, 1998.
[i]As of March 31, 1995.
[j]Funds of funds not included.

Note: Comparison of annual total assets across countries is not recommended because reporting coverage, dates, and definitions are not consistent.

Source: European Federation of Investment Funds and Companies, Investment Company Institute

Worldwide Number of Open-End Investment Companies

NON-USA COUNTRIES	1995	1996	1997	1998	1999	2000[a]
Argentina	109	149	195	229	224	226
Australia	752	1,047	488	569[b]	N/A	N/A
Austriac	452	517	625	821	1,316	1,627
Belgium	277	330	458	631	784	882
Brazil	1,172	1,143	1,502	1,601	1,760	2,082
Canada[c]	916	954	1,023	1,130	1,328	1,506
Chile	64	77	92	102	116	126[d]
Czech Republic	N/A	N/A	47	56	62	61
Denmark	168	189	222	240	304	375
Finland	44	62	81	114	176	221
France	4,878	5,379	5,797	6,274	6,511	7,065
Germany Public	583	641	717	848	895	964
Special	2,609	2,839[e]	N/A	N/A	N/A	N/A
Greece	119	148	162	179	208	248
Hong Kong	670	708	772	712	832	899
Hungary	N/A	N/A	37	66	87	90[d]
India	42	42[f]	64	97	155	221
Ireland[g]	285	260	260	260[h]	N/A	295
Italy	459	531	626	703	823	952
Japan	6,408	5,879	5,203	4,534	3,444	2,884
Korea[i]	1,943	N/A	N/A	N/A	13,606	11,677
Luxembourg	3,081	3,234	4,064	N/A	5,023	5,754
Mexico	351[j]	N/A	N/A	N/A	280	298
Netherlands[c]	161	179	289	334	348	N/A
New Zealand[c]	475	551	629	633	622	629
Norway	185	188	233	264	309	366
Philippines	N/A	N/A	N/A	N/A	15	18
Poland	4	5	20	38	62	74
Portugal	150	151	163	197	226	240
Russia	N/A	4	18	28	27	32
South Africa	91	107	149	191	260	324
Spain	743	958	1,456	1,866	2,150	2,366
Sweden	298	316	344	366	412	481
Switzerland	218	251	296	325	348	361
Taiwan	67	82[f]	127	174	318	280
United Kingdom[k]	1,490	1,452	1,455	1,541	1,594	1,799
TOTAL NON-USA	**29,264**	**28,373**	**27,614**	**25,123**	**44,625**	**45,423**
USA[k] (long-term)	4,731	5,266	5,671	6,288	6,746	6,987
(short-term)	997	988	1,013	1,026	1,045	1,040
TOTAL USA	**5,728**	**6,254**	**6,684**	**7,314**	**7,791**	**8,027**
TOTAL WORLD	**34,992**	**34,627**	**34,298**	**32,437**	**52,416**	**53,450**

[a]*As of September 30, 2000, unless otherwise noted.*
[b]*As of September 30, 1998.*
[c]*Includes real estate funds.*
[d]*As of June 30, 2000.*
[e]*As of September 30, 1996.*
[f]*As of June 30,1996.*
[g]*Approximately 95 percent relates to life assurance-linked funds; the other 5 percent are unit investment trusts.*
International Financial Service Center funds are not included.
[h]*As of March 31, 1998.*
[i]*Number of funds does not include bank trust funds.*
[j]*As of March 31, 1995.*
[k]*Funds of funds not included.*

Note: Comparison of annual total assets across countries is not recommended because reporting coverage, dates, and definitions are not consistent.

Source: European Federation of Investment Funds and Companies, Investment Company Institute

New Deposits and Outstanding Assets of Unit Investment Trusts by Type of Trust 1990-1999

(millions of dollars)

Year	Total Trusts		Equity Trusts		Taxable Debt Trusts		Tax-Free Debt Trusts	
------	New Deposits	Outstanding Assets	New Deposits	Outstanding Assets	New Deposits	Outstanding Assets	New Deposits	Outstanding Assets
1990	$7,489.1	$105,389.5	$495.4	$4,191.5	$1,349.3	$9,456.1	$5,644.4	$91,741.9
1991	8,195.3	102,827.6	899.7	4,939.5	1,686.7	9,721.0	5,608.9	88,167.1
1992	8,908.6	97,925.0	1,771.3	6,483.9	2,385.0	9,976.0	4,752.3	81,465.1
1993	9,358.7	87,573.9	3,206.0	8,494.3	1,597.7	8,566.7	4,555.1	70,512.8
1994	8,915.2	73,681.5	3,265.0	9,284.8	1,708.9	7,252.3	3,941.3	57,144.4
1995	11,264.3	73,125.1	6,743.1	14,018.7	1,154.4	8,093.7	3,366.9	51,012.7
1996	22,982.3	77,974.6	19,635.9	26,427.3	800.1	8,485.4	2,546.3	43,061.9
1997	38,521.9	86,058.5	35,885.0	42,044.7	717.5	6,480.5	1,919.4	37,533.3
1998	61,751.3	94,542.8	60,073.1	57,009.7	512.2	5,382.4	1,166.0	32,150.7
1999	75,320.1	94,602.2	73,961.5	64,760.2	286.4	4,283.3	1,072.2	25,558.7

Outstanding Assets and Number of Closed-End Funds by Type of Fund 1995-1999

(millions of dollars)

	1995 Assets Outstanding	1995 Number of Funds	1996 Assets Outstanding	1996 Number of Funds	1997 Assets Outstanding	1997 Number of Funds	1998 Assets Outstanding	1998 Number of Funds	1999 Assets Outstanding	1999 Number of Funds
Convertible	$956.8	9	$1,034.0	9	$1,151.3	10	$1,156.1	10	$1,319.5	9
Taxable Bond	26,286.9	101	26,576.4	99	26,152.1	101	32,546.9	108	27,379.6	99
Municipal Bond–National	41,383.6	96	41,113.0	94	41,944.6	99	43,032.1	103	41,926.4	106
Municipal Bond–Single State	17,540.8	106	17,406.4	104	17,802.0	101	18,851.9	108	20,636.7	132
Equity	17,741.6	49	20,297.8	47	22,303.6	48	23,455.0	48	25,254.2	50
TOTAL DOMESTIC	**103,909.7**	**361**	**106,427.6**	**353**	**109,353.6**	**359**	**119,042.0**	**377**	**116,516.4**	**396**
Multi Country Debt	1,198.1	7	2,092.8	8	2,095.7	9	1,493.7	8	1,715.7	9
Single Country Debt	1,629.4	3	2,175.8	3	2,407.5	3	1,898.1	3	1,675.5	1
Multi Country Equity	12,781.2	30	15,657.5	28	18,864.5	29	16,792.9	27	27,735.3	22
Single Country Equity	7,196.1	38	7,091.6	44	8,961.3	52	6,730.3	47	9,960.3	44
TOTAL FOREIGN	**22,804.8**	**78**	**27,017.7**	**83**	**32,329.0**	**93**	**26,915.0**	**85**	**41,086.8**	**76**
Global Debt	7,734.2	20	7,472.4	20	6,977.0	18	5,945.7	17	5,768.7	17
Global Equity	1,220.0	9	1,381.9	10	1,447.9	10	1,240.1	7	1,326.6	6
TOTAL GLOBAL	**8,954.2**	**29**	**8,854.3**	**30**	**8,424.9**	**28**	**7,185.8**	**24**	**7,095.3**	**23**
TOTAL	**135,668.7**	**468**	**142,299.6**	**466**	**150,107.5**	**480**	**153,142.8**	**486**	**164,698.5**	**495**

Data Points

	Redemptions Plus Redemption Exchanges	New Sales Plus Sales Exchanges
01/31/1991	29.6	34.1
02/28/1991	28.9	33.7
03/31/1991	28.5	33.5
04/30/1991	28.8	34.9
05/31/1991	27.9	34.0
06/30/1991	28.4	34.9
07/31/1991	27.7	35.4
08/31/1991	27.2	37.0
09/30/1991	27.8	39.3
10/31/1991	27.9	41.0
11/30/1991	28.5	42.6
12/31/1991	28.1	43.1
01/31/1992	28.2	44.0
02/29/1992	28.0	44.5
03/31/1992	28.6	45.9
04/30/1992	28.6	46.2
05/31/1992	28.0	45.9
06/30/1992	28.6	47.5
07/31/1992	28.2	47.2
08/31/1992	28.6	47.6
09/30/1992	29.0	47.8
10/31/1992	29.8	47.5
11/30/1992	29.5	47.8
12/31/1992	28.8	46.5
01/31/1993	28.1	45.9
02/28/1993	28.1	45.7
03/31/1993	28.5	46.4
04/30/1993	28.7	46.8
05/31/1993	28.6	46.6

06/30/1993	28.8	46.9
07/31/1993	28.7	46.6
08/31/1993	28.5	47.0
09/30/1993	29.0	47.4
10/31/1993	28.8	48.2
11/30/1993	30.0	48.7
12/31/1993	29.9	48.5
01/31/1994	30.1	48.7
02/28/1994	31.2	49.3
03/31/1994	34.0	50.7
04/30/1994	34.7	50.1
05/31/1994	34.6	49.0
06/30/1994	35.1	48.4
07/31/1994	34.6	46.4
08/31/1994	33.7	44.2
09/30/1994	34.1	43.7
10/31/1994	34.0	42.0
11/30/1994	35.1	41.8
12/31/1994	35.2	40.2
01/31/1995	34.5	37.5
02/28/1995	33.3	35.9
03/31/1995	32.3	35.3
04/30/1995	31.2	34.2
05/31/1995	30.9	33.8
06/30/1995	31.1	34.0
07/31/1995	30.7	33.9
08/31/1995	30.2	33.5
09/30/1995	29.8	33.6
10/31/1995	30.0	34.3
11/30/1995	29.5	35.1
12/31/1995	28.9	35.7
01/31/1996	28.8	37.1
02/29/1996	29.0	37.9
03/31/1996	28.9	38.6
04/30/1996	29.0	39.2
05/31/1996	28.7	39.4
06/30/1996	28.7	39.8
07/31/1996	29.9	40.5
08/31/1996	29.6	40.2
09/30/1996	29.0	39.4
10/31/1996	29.5	39.9
11/30/1996	28.9	39.0
12/31/1996	30.0	39.9

01/31/1997	29.9	39.4
02/28/1997	30.3	39.5
03/31/1997	31.3	40.0
04/30/1997	31.0	39.0
05/31/1997	30.0	37.6
06/30/1997	30.0	37.6
07/31/1997	29.6	38.0
08/31/1997	30.6	39.1
09/30/1997	29.8	38.2
10/31/1997	30.9	39.7
11/30/1997	30.1	39.0
12/31/1997	30.5	39.5
01/31/1998	30.0	38.6
02/28/1998	29.3	38.0
03/31/1998	29.6	38.8
04/30/1998	29.5	39.0
05/31/1998	29.5	38.9
06/30/1998	29.3	38.6
07/31/1998	29.4	38.3
08/31/1998	33.1	41.9
09/30/1998	32.5	40.4
10/31/1998	32.5	39.9
11/30/1998	32.0	38.9
12/31/1998	32.2	38.6
01/31/1999	32.6	38.9
02/28/1999	33.3	38.8
03/31/1999	33.2	38.2
04/30/1999	33.3	38.0
05/31/1999	34.7	39.0
06/30/1999	33.9	38.0
07/31/1999	34.7	38.5
08/31/1999	37.1	41.5
09/30/1999	37.1	41.4
10/31/1999	35.8	40.1
11/30/1999	35.6	39.4
12/31/1999	34.5	38.1
01/31/2000	36.0	39.6
02/29/2000	36.9	41.2
03/31/2000	37.5	41.9
04/30/2000	38.4	42.8
05/31/2000	40.1	44.5
06/30/2000	39.2	43.4
07/31/2000	40.2	44.5

08/31/2000	39.7	44.1
09/30/2000	41.0	45.7
10/31/2000	41.2	45.8
11/30/2000	42.2	46.8
12/31/2000	39.9	44.3

Page 27 — Assets of Mutual Funds, 1990-2000
(billions of dollars)

	Equity, Hybrid, and Bond Funds	Money Market Funds	Total
1990	566.9	498.3	1,065.2
1991	850.7	542.4	1,393.2
1992	1,096.3	546.2	1,642.5
1993	1,504.7	565.3	2,070.0
1994	1,544.4	611.0	2,155.4
1995	2,058.5	753.0	2,811.5
1996	2,624.5	901.8	3,526.3
1997	3,409.3	1,058.9	4,468.2
1998	4,173.5	1,351.7	5,525.2
1999	5,233.2	1,613.1	6,846.3
2000	5,120.0	1,845.3	6,965.2

Page 28 — Components of Mutual Fund Asset Growth, 1990-2000
(trillions of dollars)

	Net New Cash Flow	Performance	Newly Reporting Funds
1990	0.044	0.014	0.026
1991	0.156	0.162	0.095
1992	0.312	0.233	0.117
1993	0.539	0.391	0.159
1994	0.623	0.333	0.219
1995	0.835	0.742	0.253
1996	1.157	1.090	0.299
1997	1.531	1.637	0.320
1998	2.008	2.194	0.343
1999	2.371	3.115	0.380
2000	2.760	2.793	0.432

Page 30 — Share of U.S. Household Bond, Equity, and Short-Term Assets Held Through Mutual Funds, 1990-2000

(percent of total)

	Bonds	Equities	Short-Term Assets
1990	15.9	10.5	11.2
1991	18.6	10.5	11.7
1992	21.3	11.9	10.5
1993	25.3	15.2	10.7
1994	22.7	18.4	11.2
1995	23.9	19.6	13.5
1996	24.1	23.2	14.3
1997	26.3	24.9	15.7
1998	29.6	27.3	18.0
1999	27.9	28.1	20.0
2000	28.6	32.8	21.7

Page 33 — Interest Rate Spread and Net New Cash Flow to Retail Money Market Funds, 1991-2000

Date	Net New Cash Flow (percent of total net assets)	Interest Rate Spread (percentage points)
01/31/1991	0.932	1.17
02/28/1991	0.794	0.85
03/31/1991	0.891	0.59
04/30/1991	0.550	0.45
05/31/1991	0.165	0.30
06/30/1991	0.163	0.26
07/31/1991	(0.564)	0.28
08/31/1991	(1.022)	0.25
09/30/1991	(1.362)	0.19
10/31/1991	(1.190)	0.16
11/30/1991	(0.938)	0.14
12/31/1991	(1.273)	0.28
01/31/1992	(0.530)	0.20
02/29/1992	(0.390)	0.03
03/31/1992	(0.433)	(0.01)
04/30/1992	(0.667)	0.02
05/31/1992	(0.940)	(0.06)
06/30/1992	(0.803)	(0.09)
07/31/1992	(1.484)	0.00
08/31/1992	(1.530)	(0.08)

09/30/1992	(1.500)	(0.08)
10/31/1992	(0.930)	(0.15)
11/30/1992	(0.773)	(0.15)
12/31/1992	(0.709)	(0.04)
01/31/1993	(0.614)	(0.04)
02/28/1993	(0.461)	(0.08)
03/31/1993	(0.406)	(0.05)
04/30/1993	(0.738)	(0.03)
05/31/1993	(0.663)	(0.04)
06/30/1993	(0.599)	0.02
07/31/1993	(0.479)	0.05
08/31/1993	(0.835)	0.10
09/30/1993	(0.718)	0.15
10/31/1993	(0.653)	0.16
11/30/1993	(0.176)	0.19
12/31/1993	(0.206)	0.26
01/31/1994	(0.324)	0.24
02/28/1994	0.123	0.32
03/31/1994	0.563	0.44
04/30/1994	0.922	0.61
05/31/1994	0.313	0.86
06/30/1994	0.439	1.08
07/31/1994	0.614	1.20
08/31/1994	0.234	1.33
09/30/1994	0.047	1.50
10/31/1994	(0.097)	1.61
11/30/1994	0.574	1.82
12/31/1994	0.699	2.12
01/31/1995	0.902	2.22
02/28/1995	1.021	2.37
03/31/1995	0.921	2.39
04/30/1995	0.861	2.40
05/31/1995	0.953	2.34
06/30/1995	1.496	2.32
07/31/1995	1.498	2.24
08/31/1995	1.723	2.15
09/30/1995	1.546	2.13
10/31/1995	1.732	2.11
11/30/1995	1.529	2.10
12/31/1995	0.942	2.10
01/31/1996	0.741	2.05
02/29/1996	1.079	1.85

03/31/1996	1.261	1.85
04/30/1996	0.692	1.84
05/31/1996	0.391	1.85
06/30/1996	0.478	1.90
07/31/1996	0.820	1.93
08/31/1996	0.393	1.96
09/30/1996	0.190	1.99
10/31/1996	0.734	1.98
11/30/1996	0.951	1.99
12/31/1996	1.180	2.22
01/31/1997	0.828	2.21
02/28/1997	1.023	2.20
03/31/1997	1.455	2.09
04/30/1997	0.840	2.23
05/31/1997	0.629	2.33
06/30/1997	0.484	2.36
07/31/1997	0.528	2.38
08/31/1997	0.725	2.37
09/30/1997	0.190	2.36
10/31/1997	0.724	2.36
11/30/1997	0.894	2.43
12/31/1997	0.658	2.52
01/31/1998	0.939	2.53
02/28/1998	0.859	2.49
03/31/1998	1.336	2.47
04/30/1998	0.898	2.50
05/31/1998	1.029	2.48
06/30/1998	1.159	2.50
07/31/1998	1.085	2.49
08/31/1998	1.595	2.47
09/30/1998	1.382	2.45
10/31/1998	2.031	2.27
11/30/1998	1.862	2.24
12/31/1998	1.894	2.30
01/31/1999	1.901	2.28
02/28/1999	1.561	2.20
03/31/1999	1.587	2.22
04/30/1999	0.841	2.24
05/31/1999	0.777	2.24
06/30/1999	0.664	2.29
07/31/1999	0.560	2.42
08/31/1999	0.414	2.48

09/30/1999	0.263	2.63
10/31/1999	0.520	2.70
11/30/1999	0.800	2.83
12/31/1999	0.923	3.02
01/31/2000	1.142	3.02
02/29/2000	0.902	3.13
03/31/2000	1.335	3.28
04/30/2000	0.719	3.45
05/31/2000	0.379	3.55
06/30/2000	(0.117)	3.77
07/31/2000	(0.370)	3.86
08/31/2000	(0.404)	3.89
09/30/2000	(0.876)	3.91
10/31/2000	(0.245)	3.89
11/30/2000	0.096	3.90
12/31/2000	0.591	3.86

Page 34 — Share of U.S. Business Short-Term Assets Held Through Money Market Funds

(percent of total)

1990	8.9
1991	10.1
1992	14.6
1993	12.6
1994	13.9
1995	18.7
1996	18.0
1997	20.9
1998	28.6
1999	29.3
2000	29.0

Page 57 — Average 401(k) Account Balance by Age and Tenure, 1999

(dollars)

Age Cohort	Tenure Category (years)					
	0 to 2	>2 to 5	>5 to 10	>10 to 20	>20 to 30	> 30
20s	$4,480	$9,335	$15,589			
30s	$10,044	$18,710	$35,895	$57,001		
40s	$13,389	$23,165	$45,519	$89,258	$96,250	
50s	$15,380	$25,504	$50,945	$102,657	$149,226	$159,422
60s	$15,919	$24,084	$48,360	$96,075	$138,453	$198,595

Glossary of Mutual Fund Terms

For an explanation of fund types, see pages 3-6.

Adviser–An organization employed by a mutual fund to give professional advice on the fund's investments and asset management practices (also called the investment adviser).

After-Tax Return–The total return of a fund after the effects of taxes on distributions and/or redemptions have been assessed. Funds are required by federal securities law to calculate after-tax returns using standardized formulas based upon the highest tax rates. (Consequently, they are not representative of the after-tax returns of most mutual fund shareholders.) These standardized after-tax returns are irrelevant for shareholders in tax-deferred retirement accounts.

Annual and Semiannual Reports–Summaries that a mutual fund sends to its shareholders that discuss the fund's performance over a certain period and identify the securities in the fund's portfolio on a specific date.

Appreciation–An increase in an investment's value.

Asked or Offering Price–(As seen in some mutual fund newspaper listings, see page 14.) The price at which a mutual fund's shares can be purchased. The asked or offering price includes the current net asset value per share plus any sales charge.

Assets–The current dollar value of the pool of money shareholders have invested in a fund.

Automatic Reinvestment–A fund service giving shareholders the option to purchase additional shares using dividend and capital gain distributions.

Average Portfolio Maturity–The average maturity of all the bonds in a bond fund's portfolio.

Bear Market–A period during which securities prices in a particular market (such as the stock market) are generally falling.

Bid or Sell Price – The price at which a mutual fund's shares are redeemed, or bought back, by the fund. The bid or selling price is usually the current net asset value per share.

Bond – A debt security, or IOU, issued by a company, municipality, or government agency. A bond investor lends money to the issuer and, in exchange, the issuer promises to repay the loan amount on a specified maturity date; the issuer usually pays the bondholder periodic interest payments over the life of the loan.

Broker/Dealer (or Dealer) – A firm that buys and sells mutual fund shares and other securities from and to investors.

Bull Market – A period during which securities prices in a particular market (such as the stock market) are generally rising.

Capital Gain Distribution – Profits distributed to shareholders resulting from the sale of securities held in the fund's portfolio for more than one year.

Closed-End Fund – A type of investment company that has a fixed number of shares which are publicly traded. The price of a closed-end fund's shares fluctuates based on investor supply and demand. Closed-end funds are not required to redeem shares and have managed portfolios.

Commission – A fee paid by an investor to a broker or other sales agent for investment advice and assistance.

Compounding – Earnings on an investment's earnings. Over time, compounding can produce significant growth in the value of an investment.

Contingent Deferred Sales Charge (CDSC) – A fee imposed when shares are redeemed (sold back to the fund) during the first few years of ownership.

Credit Risk – The possibility that a bond issuer may not be able to pay interest and repay its debt.

Custodian – An organization, usually a bank, that holds the securities and other assets of a mutual fund.

Depreciation – A decline in an investment's value.

Distribution – 1) The payment of dividends and capital gains, or 2) a term used to describe a method of selling to the public.

Diversification – The practice of investing broadly across a number of securities to reduce risk.

Dollar-Cost Averaging–The practice of investing a fixed amount of money at regular intervals, regardless of whether the securities markets are declining or rising.

Exchange Privilege–A fund option enabling shareholders to transfer their investments from one fund to another within the same fund family as their needs or objectives change. Typically, fund companies allow exchanges several times a year for a low or no fee.

Exchange-Traded Fund (ETF)–An investment company with shares that trade intraday on stock exchanges at market-determined prices. Investors may buy or sell ETF shares through a broker just as they would the shares of any publicly traded company.

Ex-Dividend Date–With regard to mutual funds, this is the day on which declared distributions (dividends or capital gains) are deducted from the fund's assets before it calculates its net asset value (NAV). The NAV per share will drop by the amount of the distribution per share.

Expense Ratio–A fund's cost of doing business—disclosed in the prospectus—expressed as a percentage of its assets.

Face Value–The amount that a bond's issuer must repay at the maturity date.

Family of Funds–A group of mutual funds, each typically with its own investment objective, managed and distributed by the same company.

401(k) Plan–An employer-sponsored retirement plan that enables employees to make tax-deferred contributions from their salaries to the plan.

403(b) Plan–An employer-sponsored retirement plan that enables employees of universities, public schools, and nonprofit organizations to make tax-deferred contributions from their salaries to the plan.

457 Plan–An employer-sponsored retirement plan that enables employees of state and local governments and other tax-exempt employers to make tax-deferred contributions from their salaries to the plan.

Hedge Fund–A private investment pool for wealthy investors that, unlike a mutual fund, is exempt from SEC regulation.

Hybrid Fund–A mutual fund that invests in a combination of stocks, bonds, and other securities.

Income – Dividends, interest, and/or short-term capital gains paid to a mutual fund's shareholders. Income is earned on a fund's investment portfolio after deducting operating expenses.

Individual Retirement Account (IRA) – An investor-established, tax-deferred account set up to hold and invest funds until retirement.

Inflation Risk – The risk that a portion of an investment's return may be eliminated by inflation.

Interest Rate Risk – The possibility that a bond's or bond mutual fund's value will decrease due to rising interest rates.

Investment Adviser – An organization employed by a mutual fund to give professional advice on the fund's investments and asset management practices.

Investment Company – A corporation, trust, or partnership that invests pooled shareholder dollars in securities appropriate to the organization's objective. Mutual funds, closed-end funds, and unit investment trusts are the three main types of investment companies.

Investment Objective – The goal that an investor and mutual fund pursue together (e.g., current income, long-term capital growth, etc.).

Issuer – The company, municipality, or government agency that issues a security, such as stocks, bonds, or money market instruments.

Large-Cap Stocks – Stocks of large-capitalization companies, which are generally considered to be companies whose total outstanding shares are valued at $10 billion or more.

Liquidity – The ability to gain ready access to invested money. Mutual funds are liquid because their shares can be redeemed for current value (which may be more or less than the original cost) on any business day.

Long-Term Funds – A mutual fund industry designation for all funds other than money market funds. Long-term funds are broadly divided into equity (stock), bond, and hybrid funds.

Management Fee – The amount paid by a mutual fund to the investment adviser for its services.

Maturity – The date by which an issuer promises to repay a bond's face value.

Mutual Fund – An investment company that buys a portfolio of securities selected by a professional investment adviser to meet a specified financial goal. Investors buy shares in a fund, which represent ownership in all the fund's securities. A mutual funds stands ready to buy back its shares at their current net asset value, which is the total market value of the fund's investment portfolio, minus its liabilities, divided by the number of shares outstanding. Most mutual funds continuously offer new shares to investors.

National Association of Securities Dealers, Inc. (NASD) – A self-regulatory organization with authority over firms that distribute mutual fund shares as well as other securities.

Net Asset Value (NAV) – The per-share value of a mutual fund, found by subtracting the fund's liabilities from its assets and dividing by the number of shares outstanding. Mutual funds calculate their NAVs at least once daily.

No-Load Fund – A mutual fund whose shares are sold without a sales commission and without a 12b-1 fee of more than .25 percent per year.

Open-End Investment Company – The legal name for a mutual fund, indicating that it stands ready to redeem (buy back) its shares from investors.

Operating Expenses – Business costs paid from a fund's assets before earnings are distributed to shareholders. These include management fees, 12b-1 fees, and other expenses.

Payroll Deduction Plan – An arrangement that some employers offer employees to accumulate mutual fund shares. Employees authorize their employer to deduct a specified amount from their salaries at stated times and transfer the proceeds to the fund.

Pooling – The basic concept behind mutual funds in which a fund aggregates the assets of investors who share common financial goals. A fund uses the investment pool to buy a diversified portfolio of investments, and each mutual fund share purchased represents ownership in all the fund's underlying securities.

Portfolio – A collection of securities owned by an individual or an institution (such as a mutual fund) that may include stocks, bonds, and money market securities.

Portfolio Manager–A specialist employed by a mutual fund's adviser to invest the fund's assets in accordance with predetermined investment objectives.

Portfolio Turnover–A measure of the trading activity in a fund's investment portfolio—how often securities are bought and sold by a fund.

Prepayment Risk–The possibility that a bond owner will receive his or her principal investment back from the issuer prior to the bond's maturity date.

Principal–See Face Value.

Professional Management–The full-time, experienced team of professionals that decides what securities to buy, hold, and sell for a mutual fund portfolio.

Prospectus–The official document that describes a mutual fund to prospective investors. The prospectus contains information required by the SEC, such as investment objectives and policies, risks, services, and fees.

Quality–The creditworthiness of a bond issuer, which indicates the likelihood that it will be able to repay its debt.

Redeem–To cash in mutual fund shares by selling them back to the fund. Mutual fund shares may be redeemed on any business day. An investor receives the current share price, called net asset value, minus any deferred sales charge or redemption fee.

Redemption Price–The amount per share (shown as the "bid" in newspaper tables) that mutual fund shareholders receive when they cash in shares. The value of a fund's shares on any given day depends on the current market value of its underlying investment portfolio at that time.

Reinvestment Privilege–An option whereby mutual fund dividend and capital gain distributions automatically buy new fund shares.

Risk/Reward Tradeoff–The principle that an investment must offer higher potential returns as compensation for the likelihood of increased volatility.

Rollover–The shifting of an investor's assets from one qualified retirement plan to another—due to changing jobs, for instance—without a tax penalty.

Sales Charge or Load–An amount charged for the sale of some fund shares, usually those sold by brokers or other sales professionals. By regulation, a mutual fund sales charge may not exceed 8.5 percent of an investment purchase. The charge may vary depending on the amount invested and the fund chosen. A sales charge or load is reflected in the asked or offering price (see Asked Price).

Series Fund–A group of different mutual funds, each with its own investment objective and policies, that is structured as a single corporation or business trust.

Share Classes (e.g., Class A, Class B, etc.)–Represent ownership in the same fund, but with different fee charges. This enables shareholders to choose the type of fee structure that best suits their particular needs.

Shareholder–An investor who owns shares of a mutual fund or other company.

Short-Term Funds–Another term for money market funds.

Small-Cap Stocks–Stock of small-capitalization companies, which are generally considered to be companies whose total outstanding shares are valued at less than $1.6 billion.

Statement of Additional Information (SAI)–The supplementary document to a prospectus that contains more detailed information about a mutual fund; also known as "Part B" of the prospectus.

Stock–A share of ownership or equity in a corporation.

Total Return–A measure of a fund's performance that encompasses all elements of return: dividends, capital gain distributions, and changes in net asset value. Total return is the change in value of an investment over a given period, assuming reinvestment of any dividends and capital gain distributions, expressed as a percentage of the initial investment.

Transfer Agent–The organization employed by a mutual fund to prepare and maintain records relating to shareholder accounts.

12b-1 Fee–A mutual fund fee, named for the SEC rule that permits it, used to pay distribution costs, such as advertising and commissions paid to dealers. If a fund has a 12b-1 fee, it will be disclosed in the fee table of a fund's prospectus.

Underwriter – The organization that sells a mutual fund's shares to broker/dealers and investors.

Unit Investment Trust (UIT) – An investment company that buys and holds a fixed number of shares until the trust's termination date. When the trust is dissolved, proceeds are paid to shareholders. A UIT has an unmanaged portfolio. Like a mutual fund, shares of a UIT can be redeemed on any business day.

U.S. Securities and Exchange Commission (SEC) – The primary U.S. government agency responsible for the regulation of the day-to-day operations and disclosure obligations of mutual funds.

Variable Annuity – An investment contract sold by an insurance company; capital is accumulated, often through mutual fund investments, and converted to an income stream later, often at an investor's retirement.

Withdrawal Plan – A fund service allowing shareholders to receive income or principal payments from their fund account at regular intervals.

Yield – A measure of net income (dividends and interest) earned by the securities in a fund's portfolio less the fund's expenses during a specified period. A fund's yield is expressed as a percentage of the maximum offering price per share on a specified date.

Index

Institute Publications Order Form

Investor Awareness Series

The Institute produces a series of investor awareness publications and videotapes to help educate investors on different aspects of investing (www.ici.org/aboutfunds/investor_awareness.html).

Single copies of investor brochures ordered by commercial organizations and the general public are free of charge. Brochure quantities up to 10 are free of charge to educators, libraries, and charitable organizations, **provided that orders are received on the organization's letterhead.**

	Price	Quantity		Total
		English	Spanish	
A Guide to Mutual Funds www.ici.org/pdf/guide2mutualfunds.pdf www.ici.org/pdf/span_g2mf.pdf	35¢			
A Guide to Closed-end Funds www.ici.org/pdf/guide2closed-end.pdf www.ici.org/pdf/span_g2ce.pdf	35¢			
A Guide to Unit Investment Trusts www.ici.org/pdf/guide2uits.pdf www.ici.org/pdf/span_g2uit.pdf	35¢			
Complete set of all three Investor Brochures: *A Guide to Mutual Funds, Closed-end Funds, and Unit Investment Trusts*	90¢			
A Guide to Bond Mutual Funds www.ici.org/pdf/gd2bmf.pdf www.ici.org/pdf/span_g2bmf.pdf	35¢			
A Guide to Understanding Mutual Funds www.ici.org/pdf/g2understanding.pdf	$1.25			
Questions You Should Ask Before You Invest in a Mutual Fund www.ici.org/pdf/profile_questions.pdf	25¢			
Frequently Asked Questions About Mutual Fund Fees www.ici.org/pdf/mf_fee_faqs.pdf	50¢			

	Price	Quantity		Total
		English	Spanish	
Understanding the Role of Mutual Fund Directors www.ici.org/pdf/bro_mf_directors.pdf	50¢			
Understanding Mutual Funds (VHS videocassette and accompanying brochure)	$10			
Understanding Mutual Fund Fees and Expenses (VHS videocassette and accompanying brochure)	Free			
Facts About Funds www.ici.org/pdf/factsaboutfunds.pdf	50¢			

Industry Statistics Subscriptions

The Institute offers data subscription services to the general public. When ordering more than one of any subscription, please attach names and addresses of subscribers. All subscriptions will be billed.

	Subscription Price	Quantity	Total
Mutual Funds Statistical Report—Monthly *("Trends in Mutual Fund Activity")* Annual subscription	$400		Subscriptions will be billed
Mutual Funds Supplemental Report— *Monthly ("Backup Tables")* Annual subscription	$175		Subscriptions will be billed
Closed-End Funds Statistical Report—Annual Annual subscription	$100		Subscriptions will be billed
Unit Investment Trusts Statistical *Report—Monthly* Annual subscription	$100		Subscriptions will be billed
Institutional Shareholder Report—Annual Annual subscription	$300		Subscriptions will be billed
International Report—Quarterly Annual subscription	$300		Subscriptions will be billed
Retirement Report—Annual Annual subscription	$100		Subscriptions will be billed

Periodicals—Single Back Copies

Perspective is a series of occasional papers written by Institute staff, leading scholars, and other contributors on public policy issues of importance to mutual funds and their shareholders. A complete index of issues of *Perspective* can be found on the Institute's website at www.ici.org/economy/perspective.html.

	Price	Quantity	Total
Perspective			
Mutual Fund Assets and Flows in 2000 (Vol. 7/No. 2) www.ici.org/pdf/per07-02.pdf	$25		
401(k) Plan Asset Allocation, Account Balances, and Loan Activity in 1999 (Vol. 7/No. 1) www.ici.org/pdf/per07-01.pdf	$25		
The 1990s: A Decade of Expansion and Change in the U.S. Mutual Fund Industry (Vol. 6/No.3) www.ici.org/pdf/per06-03.pdf	$25		
Mutual Fund Assets and Flows in 1999 (Vol. 6/No. 2) www.ici.org/pdf/per06-02.pdf	$25		
401(k) Plan Asset Allocation, Account Balances, and Loan Activity in 1998 (Vol. 6/No. 1) www.ici.org/pdf/per06-01.pdf	$25		
Operating Expense Ratios, Assets, and Economies of Scale in Equity Mutual Funds (Vol. 5/No. 5) www.ici.org/pdf/per05-05.pdf	$25		
Mutual Fund Costs, 1980-1998 (Vol. 5/No. 4) www.ici.org/pdf/per05-04.pdf	$25		
Total Shareholder Cost of Bond and Money Market Mutual Funds (Vol. 5/No. 3) www.ici.org/pdf/per05-03.pdf	$25		
Mutual Fund Developments in 1998 (Vol. 5/No. 2) www.ici.org/pdf/per05-02.pdf	$25		

Fundamentals is a series of two-to-four page illustrated newsletters summarizing the findings of major Institute research projects. An index of issues of *Fundamentals* can be found on the Institute's website at www.ici.org/aboutshareholders/fundamentals.html.

	Price	Quantity	Total
Fundamentals			
Redemption Activity of Mutual Fund Owners (Vol. 10/No.1) www.ici.org/pdf/fm-v10n1.pdf	$25		
Financial Decisions at Retirement (Vol. 9/No. 6) www.ici.org/pdf/fm-v9n6.pdf	$25		
IRA Ownership in 2000 (Vol. 9/No. 5) www.ici.org/pdf/fm-v9n5.pdf	$25		
U.S. Household Ownership of Mutual Funds in 2000 (Vol. 9/No. 4) www.ici.org/pdf/fm-v9n4.pdf	$25		
Mutual Fund Shareholders' Use of the Internet (Vol. 9/No. 3) www.ici.org/pdf/fm-v9n3.pdf	$25		
Mutual Funds and the Retirement Market (Vol. 9/No. 2) www.ici.org/pdf/fm-v9n2.pdf	$25		
Use of Rule 12b-1 Fees by Mutual Funds in 1999 (Vol. 9/No. 1) www.ici.org/pdf/fm-v9n1.pdf	$25		

Shareholder Research

The Institute supports a broad program of research related to legislative and regulatory policy, economic issues, and public information. Prepayment is required on all Institute research reports.

	Price	Quantity	Total
Defined Contribution Plan Distribution Choices at Retirement: A Survey of Employees Retiring Between 1995 and 2000, Fall 2000 www.ici.org/pdf/rpt_distribution_choices.pdf	$25		
Equity Ownership in America, Fall 1999 www.ici.org/pdf/rpt_equity_owners.pdf	$25		
1998 Profile of Mutual Fund Shareholders, Summer 1999 www.ici.org/pdf/rpt_profile99.pdf	$25		
Understanding Shareholders' Use of Information and Advisers, Spring 1997 www.ici.org/pdf/rpt_undstnd_share.pdf	$25		
Mutual Fund Shareholders: The People Behind the Growth, Spring 1996 www.ici.org/pdf/rpt_peoplegrowth.pdf	$25		
Profiles of First-time Mutual Fund Buyers, Fall 1994 www.ici.org/pdf/rpt_1stbuy.pdf	$25		
Distribution Channels for Mutual Funds: Understanding Shareholder Choices, Summer 1994 www.ici.org/pdf/rpt_distrib.pdf	$25		
Understanding Shareholder Redemption Decisions, Winter 1993 www.ici.org/pdf/rpt_redempt.pdf	$25		
Piecing Together Shareholder Perceptions of Investment Risk, Spring 1993 www.ici.org/pdf/rpt_risk.pdf	$25		

Industry References

The Institute offers the following annual reference publications. *The Investment Company Service Directory* is an annual directory of paid listings and advertisements from firms that serve the fund industry. Prepayment for directory orders is required.

	Price	Quantity	Total
2001 Mutual Fund Fact Book www.ici.org/aboutfunds/factbook01_toc.html	$25		
Investment Company Service Directory	$35		
Annual Report—2000 www.ici.org/pdf/00_ici_annual.pdf	Free		

Total enclosed*

(subscriptions will be billed): _____

❏ My check for $_____ is enclosed.
(Please make checks payable to Investment Company Institute.)

❏ Charge to Visa, Mastercard, or American Express (orders of $10 or more, please):

_____

Credit Card Number   Expiration Date

_____

Name as it appears on card

_____

Signature   Today's Date

*District of Columbia addressees must add 5.75% of the total to pay Washington, DC sales tax. All payments and subscription rates include shipping and handling.

Shipping Information

Name

Title

Company

Address

City   State   Zip

Telephone

Most orders will be sent via UPS. Do not use a post office box or rural route address; UPS will not deliver to these addresses. Allow a minimum of three weeks for delivery.

Please complete and mail (check or credit card orders) or fax (credit card orders only) this form to:

Investment Company Institute
Attn: Publication Orders
1401 H Street, NW
Suite 1200
Washington, DC 20005-2148

202/326-5800

Fax: 202/326-8309

Statistical Revisions

Information in two tables was revised in the 2001 *Mutual Fund Fact Book*, 41st edition. See the specific corrections below. Replacement pages with the revised tables are also attached.

Page 64 table revisions:

The second set of column headings (located directly above the year 1984 row) should read from left to right: **Equity Funds, Hybrid Funds, Bond Funds, Taxable Money Market Funds, Tax-Exempt Money Market Funds,** and **Total.**

Page 100 table revisions:

The 2000 assets for Brazil should read **151,081.***

The Total Non-USA assets for 2000 should read **4,883,413.***

The Total World assets for 2000 should read **12,152,533.***

The 2000 assets for Hungary are as of June 30, 2000 (footnote d).

*All numbers in the page 100 table are in millions of U.S. dollars.

Total Industry Net Assets

(billions of dollars)

Year	Equity Funds	Bond & Income Funds	Taxable Money Market Funds	Tax-Exempt Money Market Funds	Total
1970	$45.1	$2.5	–	–	$47.6
1971	51.6	3.4	–	–	55.0
1972	55.9	3.9	–	–	59.8
1973	43.0	3.5	–	–	46.5
1974	30.9	3.2	$1.7	–	35.8
1975	37.5	4.7	3.7	–	45.9
1976	39.2	8.4	3.7	–	51.3
1977	34.0	11.0	3.9	–	48.9
1978	32.7	12.3	10.9	–	55.9
1979	35.9	13.1	45.2	$0.3	94.5
1980	44.4	14.0	74.5	1.9	134.8
1981	41.2	14.0	181.9	4.3	241.4
1982	53.7	23.2	206.6	13.2	296.7
1983	77.0	36.6	162.5	16.8	292.9

	Equity Funds	Hybrid Funds	Bond Funds	Taxable Money Market Funds	Tax-Exempt Money Market Funds	Total
1984	83.1	7.8	46.2	209.7	23.8	370.7
1985	116.9	12.0	122.6	207.5	36.3	495.4
1986	161.4	18.8	243.3	228.3	63.8	715.7
1987	180.5	24.2	248.4	254.7	61.4	769.2
1988	194.7	21.1	255.7	272.3	65.7	809.4
1989	248.8	31.8	271.9	358.7	69.4	980.7
1990	239.5	36.1	291.3	414.7	83.6	1,065.2
1991	404.7	52.2	393.8	452.6	89.9	1,393.2
1992	514.1	78.0	504.2	451.4	94.8	1,642.5
1993	740.7	144.6	619.5	461.9	103.4	2,070.0
1994	852.8	164.5	527.2	500.6	110.4	2,155.4
1995	1,249.1	210.5	598.9	630.0	123.0	2,811.5
1996	1,726.1	252.9	645.4	762.0	139.8	3,526.3
1997	2,368.0	317.1	724.2	898.1	160.8	4,468.2
1998	2,978.2	364.7	830.6	1,163.2	188.5	5,525.2
1999	4,041.9	383.2	808.1	1,408.7	204.4	6,846.3
2000	3,962.3	349.7	808.0	1,607.2	238.1	6,965.2

Note: The data contain a series break beginning in 1990. All funds were reclassified in 1990 and a separate category was created for hybrid funds. At the same time, data for funds that invest in other mutual funds were excluded from the series. Data prior to 1990 have been restated to create a consistent series back to 1984.

Components may not sum to the total due to rounding.

Worldwide Assets of Open-End Investment Companies
(millions of U.S. dollars)

NON-USA COUNTRIES	1995	1996	1997	1998	1999	2000[a]
Argentina	$631	$1,869	$5,247	$6,930	$6,990	$7,664
Australia	36,505	47,761	42,909	44,124[b]	N/A	328,062
Austria[c]	33,452	39,543	44,930	63,772	75,730	76,422
Belgium	25,553	29,247	33,658	56,339	65,461	65,683
Brazil	63,637	103,786	108,606	118,687	117,758	151,081
Canada[c]	107,812	154,529	197,985	213,451	269,825	287,783
Chile	2,843	2,934	4,549	2,910	4,091	4,431[d]
Czech Republic	N/A	N/A	361	556	1,473	1,754
Denmark	6,455	9,338	13,037	19,450	27,545	30,739
Finland	1,211	2,510	3,534	5,695	10,318	12,961
France	519,376	534,145	495,774	626,154	656,132	686,569
Germany Public	134,543	137,860	146,888	195,701	237,312	240,815
Special	213,047	241,642[e]	N/A	N/A	N/A	N/A
Greece	10,303	15,788	25,759	32,194	36,397	29,517
Hong Kong	33,695	41,017	58,456	98,767	182,265	222,963
Hungary	N/A	N/A	713	1,476	1,725	2,004[d]
India	10,107	9,717[f]	9,353	8,685	13,065	12,963
Ireland[g]	8,461	7,735	22,729	22,520[h]	95,135	131,160
Italy	79,878	129,992	209,410	439,701	478,530	418,874
Japan	469,980	420,103	311,335	376,533[b]	502,752	491,852
Korea	92,405	N/A	N/A	N/A	167,177	124,865
Luxembourg	285,448	338,236	390,623	N/A	659,284	727,376
Mexico	9,025[i]	N/A	N/A	N/A	19,468	19,011
Netherlands[c]	62,128	67,147	70,373	87,996	102,492	N/A
New Zealand[c]	6,868	7,686	7,519	7,250	8,502	7,258
Norway	6,834	9,930	13,058	11,148	15,107	16,195
Philippines	N/A	N/A	N/A	N/A	117	123
Poland	282	475	541	517	762	1,279
Portugal	14,233	17,079	15,472	23,299	20,574	17,005
Russia	N/A	6	41	29	177	245
South Africa	9,226	9,354	12,688	12,160	18,235	17,580
Spain	99,923	144,134	177,192	238,917	207,603	171,751
Sweden	27,388	34,981	45,452	54,923	83,250	78,989
Switzerland	44,638	48,166	53,444	69,151	82,512	82,712
Taiwan	4,388	8,351[f]	12,365	20,310	31,153	38,896
United Kingdom[j]	154,452	201,304	235,683	283,711	370,962	376,831
TOTAL NON-USA	**2,574,727**	**2,816,365**	**2,769,684**	**3,143,056**	**4,569,879**	**4,883,413**
USA[j] (long-term)	2,058,466	2,624,463	3,409,315	4,173,531	5,233,194	5,541,430
(short-term)	753,018	901,807	1,058,886	1,351,678	1,613,145	1,727,690
TOTAL USA	**2,811,484**	**3,526,270**	**4,468,201**	**5,525,209**	**6,846,339**	**7,269,120**
TOTAL WORLD	**$5,386,211**	**$6,342,635**	**$7,237,885**	**$8,668,265**	**$11,416,218**	**$12,152,533**

[a]As of September 30, 2000, unless otherwise noted.

[b]As of September 30, 1998.

[c]Includes real estate funds.

[d]As of June 30, 2000.

[e]As of September 30, 1996

[f]As of June 30, 1996

[g]Approximately 95 percent relates to life assurance-linked funds; the other 5 percent are unit investment trusts. International Financial Service Center funds are not included.

[h]As of March 31, 1998.

[i]As of March 31, 1995.

[j]Funds of funds not included.

Note: Comparison of annual total assets across countries is not recommended because reporting coverage, dates, and definitions are not consistent.

Source: European Federation of Investment Funds and Companies, Investment Company Institute

INVESTMENT
COMPANY
INSTITUTE®

1401 H Street, NW
Suite 1200
Washington, DC 20005-2148
202/326-5800

www.ici.org